Journey to American Samoa

JOURNEY TO AMERICAN SAMOA

Peter W Noonan

MAGISTRALIS

Ottawa, Canada

Journey to American Samoa Copyright © 2024 by Peter W Noonan. All Rights Reserved.

Print ISBN: 978-1-7780030-4-2 (softcover perfect bound)

E-Book ISBN: 978-1-7780030-5-9

Cataloguing in Publication Data may be obtained from:

Library and Archives Canada
395 Wellington Street
Ottawa ON Canada K1A 0N4

Cover Design: Kate McDonnell

Contents

Author's Note
vii

Image Credits
viii

American Samoa - The Basics
1

Part I.
Main Body

Chapter 1.
Travel Plans
7

Chapter 2.
Where We Stayed
12

Chapter 3.
The People of American Samoa
18

Chapter 4.
The Culture of American Samoa
20

Chapter 5.
The Preeminence of Religion
29

Chapter 6.
A Basic History of American Samoa
31

Chapter 7.
Central Tutuila
49

Chapter 8.
The Coastal Road East
71

Chapter 9.
The Coastal Road West
84

Chapter 10.
The National Park of American Samoa
91

Chapter 11.
A Visit to Government House
102

Chapter 12.
The Islands We Missed -- The Outer Islands
122

Chapter 13.
Departing American Samoa
127

The Present and Future of American Samoa
129

Author's Note

What follows is an account of a journey to American Samoa in the winter of 2024.

Image Credits

All photographs in this book are credited to the author with the following exceptions

Page 36: *HHMS Kaimiloa* firing a salute at Samoa (Wikimedia Commons: Kaimiloa PNLPC-3-07577 jpg., public domain)

Page 39: *Staatssekretar Solf* at her launch in 1914 (Wikipedia.de: Deutsche Kolonialzitung. 31. Jg. (1914), Ausg. Nr. 4 vom 24. Januar 1914, S. 57.)

Page 105: Government House (Wikimedia Commons: Government House or Governor's Mansion. jpg, Roy G. Klotz M.D., Creative Commons Attribution-Share Alike 3.0)

Page 123: Ofu Beach (Wikimedia Commons: Ofu Beach American Samoa, US National Park Service. jpg, public domain)

American Samoa - The Basics

American Samoa consists of the eastern islands of the Samoan Archipelago in the South Pacific Ocean. Its geographical coordinates are 14 degrees and 20 minutes South and 170 degrees and zero minutes West. Generally speaking, the islands lie roughly one-half of the distance between Hawaii and New Zealand. They constitute the only inhabited sovereign possession of the United States of America that lies south of the equator. American Samoa consists of the island of Tutuila, upon which most of the population of the country resides, Tutuila's small neighbour, Aunu'u Island, and further east the Manu'a Islands of Ta'u, Ofu, and Olosega. In addition, there are two small atolls, Rose Atoll, which is the southernmost limit of American sovereignty in the South Pacific, and Swains Island in the north, which is geographically part of the Tokelau Islands but is politically part of American Samoa. All of the islands of American Samoa are mountainous islands of volcanic origin, except for Rose Atoll and Swains Island.

American Samoa's closest neighbour is the Independent State of Samoa ('Samoa') formerly called Western Samoa, which lies northwest of American Samoa. Samoa and American Samoa share the Samoan Archipelago and the same language and culture. Farther afield, the more remote neighbours of American Samoa are the Tokelau Islands to the north, Niue to the south, the Cook Islands to the east, and Tonga to the southwest.

In total area, American Samoa consists of 224 square kilometres of land and has a combined total area (land and water) of slightly above 300,000 square kilometres. It is a beautiful land of sharp-tipped mountains covered by rainforests that are filled with trees and ferns, and it enjoys a warm tropical climate caressed by the southeast trade winds. There is little variation in temperature across its two annual seasons, one dry and the other wet. The islands are ringed by white sand beaches and the shallow warm seas of the coastal South Pacific.

Tutuila is the main island in the American Samoan group and it is a significant mountainous island approximately 30 kilometres in length and six kilometres in width. Two coastal plains, in the south, the Tafuna Plain, and the Leone Plain, hold most of the island's population of about 43,000 people. The total population of the whole country is 44,620. Tutuila is famed for the superb natural harbour at Pago Pago (pronounced 'Pango Pango,' because the 'g' in the Samoan language is pronounced as 'ng'). Indeed, it was the attraction of this harbour that first drew the United States to the Samoan Archipelago. Visiting US Navy officers quickly realised the strategic importance of the harbour at Pago Pago for naval operations in the Pacific Ocean. The harbour is lorded over by Rainmaker Mountain, which is also called Mount Pioa and is responsible for forcing clouds to drench the harbour with an annual rainfall of 3256 mm, giving Pago Pago Harbour the record for receiving the greatest amount of precipitation of any harbour in the world.

The magnificent harbour at Pago Pago

American Samoa is an overseas territory of the United States. Constitutionally it is considered to be an unincorporated and unorganised territory of the United States. As an unincorporated territory, American Samoa is not eligible to become a state in the American Union because only incorporated territories are eligible for admission to the American Union as a state.

The central US government has never legislated a form of government for American Samoa. These islands were governed by US Navy officers for the first half of the twentieth century. Following the departure of the naval officers in the 1950s, the inhabitants were pretty much left to their own devices to establish a form of government that best suited them, and so the islanders adopted a constitution of their own making for American Samoa in 1960. Outwardly, the form of the American Samoan government parallels the forms of American government but there are also significant differences.

The country's head of state is the President of the United States for the time being, whose responsibilities concerning the governance of American Samoa are discharged by the US Secretary of the Interior through the Office of Insular Affairs in the Department of the Interior. The President is elected by the people of the US mainland and not by American Samoans. American Samoans do not have the right to participate in presidential elections (although they are permitted to participate in presidential nominating contests). The President appoints the Secretary of the Interior, subject to confirmation by the US Senate, a body which does not have a representative from American Samoa.

The head of government of American Samoa is the Governor, who is popularly elected by the people of American Samoa every four years in a territorial election. There is also a Lieutenant Governor who is popularly elected in conjunction with the Governor, and who can exercise executive authority if the Governor is away from the territory, or is unable to exercise the functions of his or her office.

Laws are passed by a bicameral legislature called the *Fono*. The *Fono* consists of a lower House of Representatives that possesses 21 members of whom 20 are popularly elected and one, a non-voting representative from Swains Island, is selected by a local consensus. Members of the House of Representatives serve for a term of two years. There is also a Senate of 18 members who are appointed by the *Matai*, the village chiefs, and the high chiefs, who hold traditional power in Samoan society. Senators serve for a term of four years.

One person is also popularly elected to serve a two-year term as a non-voting delegate from American Samoa to the US House of Representatives in Washington, D.C.

Villages are administered through a village *Fono* led by a village *Matai*. The village political structure connects the local *Matai* to the country's executive through a system of district governors who are appointed by the Governor of American Samoa.

A unique feature of American Samoa that is not present in the United States, or its other territories, is the continued use of indigenous aristocratic titles as a measure of individual status in society. (For example, the current Governor in 2024 holds the title Lemanu.) When Germany and the United States partitioned the islands in 1899, they abolished the previous indigenous monarchy. However, the aristocracy that supported the monarchical structure was not abolished, and that system, which is tied into the *Matai* structures in both American Samoa and in Samoa, continues today. Thus, leaders of an *aiga*, or family group, are ennobled in titling ceremonies, and their aristocratic titles are registered in court and are acknowledged and respected by other American Samoans. There is a particular ranking of titles within the American Samoan aristocracy such that some nobles hold more revered titles than others.

As a result of its peculiar constitutional position the inhabitants of American Samoa are not US citizens but rather have the status of American Nationals. As American Nationals people born in American Samoa owe allegiance to the United States but they do not enjoy US citizenship. The United States Constitution applies to them only partially, and then only in respect of the fundamental rights enjoyed by all individuals under the US Constitution. As American Nationals, American Samoans have both a right of entry and a right of abode within the United States, and they cannot be deported or excluded.

Despite the peculiarities of its relationship with the United States, the islanders enjoy certain advantages in not being an incorporated and organised territory, or in holding US citizenship. Due to their separate constitutional status, American Samoans can pass and maintain local laws that support, rather than undermine, their own national culture, and therefore laws concerning land ownership, religious institutions, and the manner of selecting persons for political offices can and do differ from the comparable laws applicable to Americans living on the US mainland. American Samoa maintains its own separate customs and immigration jurisdictions, and it sets its own requirements for the admission of people and goods into the territory. American Samoa also assesses its own income tax on residents.

There is a court structure for the territory that applies common law and customary Samoan law. At the apex is the High Court of Justice of American Samoa with both trial and appellate divisions. The Chief Justice and the Associate Chief Justice of the High Court are appointed by the Secretary of the Interior in Washington while six puisne Justices are appointed by the Governor of American Samoa. All Justices serve on the court for life. There is also a system of district courts for minor civil and criminal matters and village courts that apply traditional village rules.

1

Travel Plans

American Samoa lies far away from North America so it was no easy feat to plan a trip there for my wife Vi and me. While some visitors arrive from Samoa or Tonga, North American visitors will generally arrive in one of three ways: by air via Hawaiian Airlines from Honolulu, by cruise ship on trans-Pacific itineraries, or by private yacht. For us, air was the only viable option. American Samoa generally follows the United States in permitting the citizens of certain countries, including Canada, where we live, to enter without obtaining a visa but all visitors, including US citizens, must obtain an entry permit to American Samoa called an 'OK to Board' before embarking on any mode of transport to American Samoa. The OK to Board is granted upon application by the American Samoa Department of Legal Affairs and requires some basic information about a visitor and the purpose of their visit to American Samoa. If a visitor does not obtain an OK to Board, they will be denied admission to the country.

Our journey began near the end of January 2024, when we caught a Via Rail Canada intercity train from our home in Ottawa,

Ontario, to Dorval, which is a suburb of Montreal, Quebec. After alighting from the train in Dorval we boarded a quick shuttle service over to Montreal - Pierre Trudeau International Airport. There, we caught a five-and-one-half-hour Air Canada flight from Montreal to Vancouver, British Columbia. We arrived in Vancouver in the evening and rested at a business traveller hotel near the airport. The next morning we caught another Air Canada flight from Vancouver International Airport to Honolulu, Hawaii, where we arrived following a six-hour flight in the early afternoon. In Honolulu, we checked into the Ala Moana Hotel, which is adjacent to Waikiki for a single night. That gave us a brief opportunity to visit the Bishop Museum in Honolulu. The Bishop Museum contains the largest collection of Polynesian artifacts in the world and we explored the museum's fine collection of Polynesian materials, including objects from the Samoan culture.

Samoan headdress at the Bishop Museum

By late afternoon we were back at the Daniel K. Inouye International Airport in Honolulu where we prepared for our flight to Pago Pago in American Samoa. Our flight on Hawaiian Airlines to Pago Pago was aboard an Airbus A-330 aeroplane departing in the late afternoon. At the airport waiting area in the modern wing of the airport and on the aeroplane itself we had our first introduction to the people of American Samoa, as most of our fellow passengers were returning to the islands. We were struck by the substantial stature of many of our fellow passengers. Like the Polynesians of old, many of them were tall and broad-shouldered, with some possessing substantial girth. Some of the men on the flight were so substantial in physical stature that

I wondered whether they could be football players. The American football season had recently ended for both the professional and college leagues (except for the professional championship Super Bowl game) and I thought that some of the men travelling back to American Samoa on our flight might have been football players, as it is well known that American Samoans have had successful football careers in the United States. Certainly, looking around I felt that these were not the kind of men that I would want to have a serious disagreement with! However, I would soon learn that American Samoans were invariably polite and friendly people, even if some of the men looked like they could break another person in half!

When boarding our aeroplane the Hawaiian Airlines staff asked for and checked my OK to Board document but my wife, who is originally from southeast Asia, apparently passed for an American Samoan so she was not asked to produce her OK to Board. Our Hawaiian Airlines flight was four hours in duration, departing at 4:40 P.M. and arriving at Pago Pago International Airport on the main American Samoan island of Tutuila at around 9:30 in the evening. The flight was pleasant and we enjoyed a complimentary food service - something that is now rare on North American Airlines. I occupied myself on the flight by watching a recent Tom Hanks movie called 'Finch.' It was a surprisingly moving story about a computer scientist in a post-apocalyptic world who constructed and trained an artificially intelligent robot to care for his beloved dog in the knowledge that the scientist would soon be no more.

It was dark as our plane began its final approach into Pago Pago International Airport and as we drew close to landing I overheard a young American Samoan woman behind me who must have been returning home after an absence ask someone in a window seat if they could see the lights of the island. Upon receiving an affirmative answer she softly said "Hello Samoa - long time no see."

It was a warm summer night as we walked down the mobile steps from the aeroplane to the ground (in the southern hemisphere the summer months correspond to the winter months in the northern hemisphere). As with any international arrival, there are procedures to complete and forms to fill out before gaining admission to a country, and American Samoa was no different. We went first through a line staffed by Public Health officials who questioned us about COVID-19 symptoms and took down the details of where we staying on the island of Tutuila. They also gave each of us a COVID-19 test kit with an explanation that COVID-19 was present on the island. Of course, we were up to date with our COVID-19 vaccinations so we had no particular concern about the disease but I was struck by the fact that American Samoa was still taking COVID-19 very seriously even though the pandemic had now ended, and life everywhere else was pretty much back to normal. Still, I was impressed by this country's continuing precautionary approach.

Next, we lined up for Immigration control and reported who we were, and the purpose of our visit (tourism) to a serious-looking middle-aged man who closely inspected our Canadian passports and took our OK to Board documents. Satisfied, he stamped our passports with admission visas and we proceeded through a slightly chaotic airport scene to collect our luggage. The arrivals area was filled with residents welcoming back loved ones and others who had been travelling outside the islands. Once we retrieved our luggage we proceeded through American Samoan customs and then we found ourselves outside in the night air amidst many more greetings for returning residents from the locals.

We quickly located a shuttle bus that would take us to the hotel where we would be staying and soon we were on our way through the darkened streets of Tafuna to our hotel.

2

Where We Stayed

American Samoa is not a popular tourist destination and it possesses none of the elaborate resort accommodations one can find elsewhere in the Pacific region. Nor are there any of the mega-chain hotels catering to tourists that one would find in Hawaii or on the North American mainland. That said, there is a range of pleasant accommodations of varying types that are available to suit the tastes of visitors who do come to American Samoa. While preparing for our trip we wrote to the American Samoa Visitors Bureau for information about the islands, and they sent us a package of materials, including brochures from several of the local hotels, including the Tradewinds Hotel, the Turtle and Shark Lodge, Sadie's by the Sea, and the Sadie Thomson Inn. While all of them appeared to have particular advantages we chose to stay at the Tradewinds Hotel in the Ottoville District of Tafuna because it was relatively close to the stores we thought we might need, and it was also reasonably close to the Greater Pago Pago urban area. This was a trip where we would not be spending much beach time so we also thought that a seaside hotel was not necessary.

The Tradewinds Hotel, Tafuna

The Sadie Thomson Inn, an older establishment in Pago Pago has a certain notoriety that some visitors may find attractive. It is said to be the setting of a story called *Rain* by the well-known twentieth-century British author Somerset Maugham. His short story details the interaction (perhaps collision is a better word) between a missionary and a visiting prostitute in Pago Pago in the early twentieth century. Maugham wrote the fictional story while he and his travelling companion were ensconced in a guest house in Pago Pago waiting out a quarantine period. Today the guest house where he wrote the story is operated as the Sadie Thomson Inn. Western literary aficionados may beat a path to the inn simply because of Maugham's story but it is hard to believe that the locals would have much truck with promoting it, as American Samoan society is quite religious.

The Turtle and Shark Inn on the other hand is a nod to a famous American Samoan legend about a grandmother and granddaughter who were shunned by their family and who were forced by famine to throw themselves into the sea where they were transformed into a turtle and a shark. They were said to have travelled as sea creatures to Tutuila, where they reverted to human form and were received and cared for by a village. Out of gratitude, they promised that when they returned to the sea they would always protect the village.

However, having chosen the Tradewinds Hotel I can say that we liked it. It was a comfortable business-type hotel with all the basics including a restaurant, tuck shop, a beautiful swimming pool, and it provided us with a spacious and comfortable room with a small refrigerator and a microwave. Tradewinds is the place that US officials from the mainland stay at when they come to American Samoa on government business (and its room rates are priced accordingly). Among the other guests or visitors that we saw during our stay were US Coast Guard officers in their summer whites, US Army or marine soldiers in their green fatigues, and a variety of well-dressed business people in the company of some of the Samoan movers and shakers in the local commercial and government worlds.

The Koi Pond at the Tradewinds Hotel

The hotel staff were pleasant and the hotel grounds were attractive and well-kept. Our room overlooked the back gardens of the hotel where there was a stone path through a collection of tropical and flowering plants. Farther away there was a tranquil fish pond filled with young koi fish. Smack in the middle of the rear garden was a large and attractive swimming pool surrounded by a large patio. The Equator Restaurant provided the basic business-hotel fare in a small but comfortable setting. The adjacent Equator Bar supplied libations of choice and it attracted a mostly American expat crowd on weekends. We did experience one minor disappointment at the hotel. We inquired about a traditional Samoan dance spectacle, including a *Siwa* dance, which we had heard was offered by the Equator Restaurant in the hotel on Friday nights. Unfortunately, we were told that it was no longer being offered by the hotel.

A curious incident at our hotel occurred on a Sunday afternoon after we had returned after a long drive. The hotel pool looked quite inviting to me as I looked out of our room. I saw several adults together with their children and some youths sitting on the edge of the swimming pool idly swinging their legs in it without swimming. A single small child was floating on a floater very close to its mother at the side of the pool. All of the people appeared to be either Samoans or some other Pacific Islander ethnicity.

The Swimming Pool at the Tradewinds Hotel

I thought that I might as well go down for a dip in the pool so I put on my swimming trunks and made my way down to the poolside where I showered briefly and then went into the pool for a satisfying swim. Tradewinds has a strikingly large outdoor pool and the water was warm and inviting though I noted that the water came right up to the lip of the pool, a fact that I attributed to the recent rains that we had experienced the night before. Soon, following my example, all of the people who were sitting on the side of the pool when I came down to the pool deck slowly began to enter the water.

After swimming for a while I got out and sat on a plastic pool chair to dry off in the sunshine. As I did so a man who had been swimming came up to me and said "Thanks for setting the trend." Perplexed, I asked, "What Trend?" He explained that the people sitting on the side of the pool were part of a large family from Hawaii visiting Tutuila for a family funeral. They had not gone into the pool because the hotel staff had come out and told them that the pool was closed for 'safety reasons.' He could not fathom what safety issue was present unless it was the fact that the water level was up close to the lip of the pool but once I ventured into the pool everyone was happy to follow my example. A mature woman overheard our conversation and also called out to me; "Yes! Thanks for setting the trend." I laughingly replied that it was the first time in my life that I had set a trend for anything but I was happy to have done so, seeing how the children and youths especially were enjoying themselves in the pool. Since the hotel staff had not stopped me from entering, and there was no signage forbidding swimming, I had just assumed that the pool was open for anyone who wanted to swim.

Although the hotel staff probably thought that the slight increase in the water level presented a danger to some swimmers I wondered if the conservative views of Samoan society around Sunday observances might have also influenced them. Regardless, my example led to enjoyment for the other guests, and for the remainder of the day and into the early evening I listened to the lively sounds of children, youths, and adults immersing themselves in the pleasures of the pool.

3

The People of American Samoa

The people of American Samoa are Polynesians. In Oceania, ethnographers divide the Pacific into three ethnographic areas, Polynesia, Melanesia, and Micronesia. Polynesians inhabit the myriad of islands bounded by the Hawaiian Islands to the north, Easter Island to the east, and New Zealand to the south, thus forming a large triangle on the surface of the Pacific Ocean. Polynesians are typically a large and muscular group with light brown skin and dark, somewhat wavy hair. The Samoan Islands have traditionally been viewed as the very heart of Polynesia and there has been much less racial mixing among the Samoans so they are currently viewed as having the most consistent Polynesian bloodlines over time. Despite some physical differences between Polynesian, Melanesian, and Micronesian populations all Pacific Islanders, together with the indigenous inhabitants of maritime southeast Asia (Indonesia, Malaysia, Taiwan, and the Philippines) are linguistically identifiable as members of the Austronesian language group. Therefore, linguistic and even cultural connections exist between the peoples of southeast Asia, particularly those residing in the Asian maritime littoral region, and the peoples of the Pacific islands. In American Samoa, the local population speaks the Samoan language although practically everyone is bilingual Samoan/English so it is very easy for visitors from North America to navigate their way around the islands.

As American Nationals, people born in American Samoa have the right to relocate to the US mainland, or Hawaii, and large numbers of American Samoans are now to be found in the Hawaiian Islands or the continental United States. Outward migration has resulted in population fluctuations within the country. However, there have been considerable influxes of immigrants from the neighbouring islands of Samoa, who integrate easily into American Samoa owing to the commonality of the Samoan culture and language. Thus, there is an overall stability in the population of the country, with inflows of people from Samoa replenishing the population that migrates to the United States.

4

The Culture of American Samoa

The culture of American Samoa is strongly Samoan, supplemented by a veneer of American culture.

The Bedrock of Tradition - *Fa'a Samoa*

On Tutuila, archaeological excavations have shown that American Samoa has been populated for more than 3000 years. Throughout time, the Samoans have been able to preserve their culture to a much greater degree than other Polynesian islands. *Fa'a Samoa* (the Samoan Way) rigorously commands the adherence of the local population to custom and tradition. The centre of Samoan life is the *aiga*, which is the extended family. Generally, the larger the *aiga* the more socially prominent a particular person is in Samoan society. Each *aiga* is led by a *Matai*, or chief, who represents the *aiga* in the village *Fono*, or council, which is the basic unit of local government. The village *Fono*, is presided over by a high chief. The *Matai* is recognized or selected by the members of each *aiga* and they can be either male or female, although males predominate. All members of an *aiga* owe lifetime service to it, and that lifetime service is called *tautua*.

The Samoans are a collectivist culture meaning that individualism is subordinated to the needs and interests of the group (e.g., an *aiga*, or the village, etc.). Landholding in American Samoa is communal for the most part (and private land sales are only possible in Tafuna, where most of the expat community resides). As a corollary to this collectivist approach, the needs of all members of society are addressed within each *aiga*. Thus the aged and infirm are cared for by members of their *aiga* and any orphans are quickly adopted within the *aiga*. Children must show respect to adults and must obey them. Age is important in Samoan society and respect for elders is a key aspect of the local culture. Owing to the communal landholding structure, upon death members of the *aiga* are interred on communal lands where the members of their *aiga* reside. Thus, many residential properties contain graves. The old naval cemetery called Satala on the east side of Pago Pago Harbour is the only public cemetery.

For the responsible travellers there are established rules in a traditional society that must be followed and we made sure to do some research on what to expect before visiting these islands. Modest dress is important in this Samoan society, and although Western beachwear is acceptable on the beach it is not considered acceptable in villages, and covering up after exiting the water is expected. When visiting a Samoan residence one must remove footwear before entering (which is, of course, also a North American custom) and one must not stand inside a home when elders are present and are seated. When seated on a floor, or mat, one should sit with one's legs crossed or else place your legs to the side. And one must never point their feet at a person! In addition, there is some sensitivity concerning photographs and permission should be sought from a local adult person if a visitor wishes to take photographs inside a village. Finally, certain *aigas* have some proprietary control over beach access in villages so permission should be obtained from a responsible person before using a beach in a village, or one that is adjacent to a residential property. A small donation may also be required for the use of a beach.

Vi found some of these customs to be quite familiar to her because the same customs could also be found in Laos, where she was born. In particular, modest dress in villages, sitting cross-legged on mats, and never pointing your feet at someone are also traditional customs in Southeast Asia, as is the imperative of showing respect to one's elders. Certainly, we had no difficulty complying with any of these customs during our visit to this country.

But it begs the question; Doesn't *Fa'a Samoa* feel confining to the people who live here? In my brief exposure to the culture, I would say probably not for most people although I did meet one person who said that they found it constricting. For most American Samoans however, *Fa'a Samoa* is central to their way of life and their culture. And I suppose that those who would find it confining have a choice. They can stay and accept it or they can exercise their rights as American Nationals to relocate to Hawaii, or the US mainland, and adopt a more Western lifestyle.

Architectural Styles

Traditional architecture in the Samoan islands is represented by the *Fale*, a type of oval structure consisting of a series of wood posts holding up a deep upside-down bowl-shaped roof of thatch. There are no walls attached to a *Fale* and the structure is open to the elements although where a *Fale* is used as a residence mats can be fixed to the roof support and those can be lowered for visual privacy. The traditional *Fale* has now largely disappeared from American Samoa however, and most housing in the country now consists of variations of western-style housing. Nevertheless, the *Fale* design has been retained for ceremonial and community meeting purposes, albeit now made with modern materials. Thus, the traditional *Fale* style can be seen in most communities on the islands, though it no longer forms the preferred housing style. Modern *Fale* may be round, rectangular, or oval in shape and are now roofed with more permanent roofing materials.

A Community Fale

Ava Ceremonies

An important part of any ceremony in most parts of Polynesia is the preparation and serving of a special refreshment called *Ava* in Samoa and *Kava* elsewhere in Polynesia. *Ava* is a slightly narcotic drink that is prepared from the root of the pepper plant. The selected roots are first scraped or pounded into a mash in a bowl containing water and then strained. The resulting liquid is then placed in a ceremonial vessel and offered to important guests, generally in their order of precedence taking into account political positions and aristocratic titles. At a formal *Ava* ceremony, it is also quite customary for speeches to be made.

A ceremonial vessel made of coconut that may be used for refreshments

Gifts of the Women

Important events such as a marriage, a funeral, or an ennoblement ceremony in which a person receives an aristocratic title, call for the presentation of a special gift, a finely woven mat called an *ie toga*. Such mats are made from pandanus fibres cut into two-millimetre widths and then woven together. That is time-consuming and very detailed work and fewer and fewer women possess the skill to make those mats. Women in American Samoa also make a bark cloth from the inner bark of the mulberry plant called *siapo*, on which geometric patterns are painted. These objects, the *ie toga* and the *siapo* are known as the 'gifts of the women' in Samoan society and we were told that it is absolutely essential for gifts of this kind to be given at important social occasions. A failure to provide them can result in a person losing face in a societal judgement. Interestingly, there is also a category of 'gifts of the men,' which men are required to provide but the men's gifts only consist of gifts of easy-to-obtain agricultural products.

A Samoan Siapo

Detail from the Siapo above

The Art of the Tatoo

Tattooing is a very important part of Samoan society, especially for males. The art of tattoos has existed in Samoan society continuously since ancient days, having been brought to these islands from Fiji by two sisters, according to legend. The art of tattoos was never suppressed here as it was in other Polynesian societies by Christianity. A *Pe'o* is a male tattoo that covers the male body between the waist and the knees. It is still practised using traditional tools such as shark teeth and boar tusks, although modern tools and techniques are also used today. The *Malu* is the female tattoo that covers the female thigh. The tattoo procedure, especially for males can take a few weeks and it is painful, especially when traditional tools are used. However, once commenced, it is regarded as a mark of shame if a man does not see the process through to completion.

The Art of Dance

As in other Pacific island cultures, dance is an important element of expression. A *Fiafia* was originally a costumed play or musical in Samoan society but today in American Samoa a *Fiafia* is a fine traditional dance to the beat of drums, although the costumed variety may still be offered on important social occasions. A *Fiafia* dance usually ends with the *Siwa* dance, a slow and flowing dance performed by a young woman of considerable social stature, such as the daughter of a *Matai*. The famous Fire Knife Dance seen elsewhere in Polynesia and which is a staple at Hawaiian tourist luaus is said to have originated in the Samoan Islands and it is performed by men at night. Men also perform a type of thigh-slapping dance.

Sports in American Samoa

Sports are important to American Samoans and the most popular sports are a mix of American and British sports. Cricket seemed to us to be the most visibly popular sport and we saw quite a few teams participating in weekend Cricket matches, all displaying their team colours. We saw both male and female teams playing this sport. Although we did not see anyone playing baseball or softball, we were told that the sport was played on the islands. Another very popular sport is American football and we saw plenty of evidence of American Samoan's love for America's game. A higher proportion of American Samoans play football on the US mainland than any other American state or territory. During our visit the 2024 Super Bowl game was upcoming and we saw local fans displaying the colours of their preferred teams. By my rough estimate, American Samoans preferred the San Francisco 49ers over the Kansas City Chiefs but alas for the local fans, the Kansas City team eked past the 49ers to win the title. European football, what is called soccer in North America, seems much less popular but a movie was recently made about American Samoa's erstwhile national soccer team so perhaps with the publicity it might grow in the country. A very traditional sport that is part of the culture of American Samoa is racing canoes, and, in particular the *Fautasi* racing canoe, which can seat up to 45 rowers at a time.

Beauty Competitions

As in some other smaller countries in the Pacific and elsewhere, there is an important place for female beauty contests. The Miss American Samoa contest results in the participation of a representative of American Samoa in the larger Miss Pacific Islands beauty pageant, which brings together representatives from several Pacific island countries. Past winners of the Miss American Samoa contest have gone on to win the Miss Pacific Islands Contest several times. Locally, Miss American Samoa acts as a tourism ambassador, and she makes public appearances at events in American Samoa.

American Samoa in Literature and Film

There is a paucity of literature concerning American Samoa, especially indigenous literature. Most of what has been written about the place has been from the perspective of outsiders.

Of the books and stories that have been written about or concerning American Samoa one or two particularly stand out. The

British author Somerset Maugham wrote a celebrated story set in American Samoa entitled *Rain*, the story of a prostitute and of the missionary who sought to reform her. It was written while Maugham was stranded in Pago Pago in 1916 due to a quarantine issue and it was based on characters that he sailed into the islands with. The popularity of *Rain* led to it being made into a motion picture in the 1930s starring Joan Crawford, following an earlier silent film release in the 1920s starring Gloria Swanson. A 1950s remake starring Rita Hayworth entitled *Miss Sadie Thompson* was weakened by the strong censorship of that era. A very recent motion picture about American Samoa that we watched at a cinema before travelling to Tutuila is *Next Goal Wins*, a feel-good Hollywood flick about the trials and tribulations of the national soccer team of American Samoa. The movie starring Richard Fassbender has its charms, and it does portray some of the unique cultural customs of American Samoa although sadly it was actually filmed in Hawaii.

There is a movie theatre on Tutuila that plays first-run movies and there is also television representing the main American television networks, as well as Christian television programming and independent television. Eleven radio stations broadcast in American Samoa, on Tutuila, and in the Manu'a Islands.

Of nonfiction literature, the most famous book with an American Samoan connection is *Coming of Age in Samoa* by the noted American cultural anthropologist Margaret Mead. Written in the early twentieth century her book argued that adolescents in American Samoa suffered less stress growing up than their counterparts in North America. Her research contributed to anthropological debates about the varying impacts of civilization and natural states on adolescent development.

5

The Preeminence of Religion

Religion, and here I speak of Christianity, is of paramount importance in Samoan society. Christian missionaries came to Samoa in 1830 and thereafter Christianity supplanted the older, traditional religious systems. Today, Christianity dominates Samoan life in the islands and 98% of the population profess to be Christians. Many villages in American Samoa still practice evening vespers, which are known locally as *Sa*. A bell, or gong struck in the late afternoon brings village life to a halt for a quarter-hour of prayer and, as visitors, we were warned not to walkabout in any villages practising *Sa* while *Sa* was underway.

Sunday is of special importance and almost everything shuts down on Tutuila so that its inhabitants can honour the Lord's Day. Most people attend Sunday services dressed in their best Sunday clothes, a long white dress and a hat for women and dark trousers and a white shirt for men. Sunday services are usually followed in Samoan households by a family feast. The entire day is set aside as a day of rest to be spent with family and in most villages entertainments are not permitted, including swimming at a beach. We were warned that even hiking may be frowned upon and that it would not be wise to hike on a Sunday, although a Sunday drive was unobjectionable.

A Church in American Samoa

American Samoa has a large number of churches, as one would expect to find in a society with a strong religious tradition, and it seemed to us as if there was one church every few kilometres. The churches were always the most impressive edifices in the villages that we visited.

6

A Basic History of American Samoa

The islands of American Samoa have been inhabited for about 3000 years according to archeological investigations conducted on Tutuila, at Tula, and in Aoa. A similar time frame applies to the Manu'a Islands based on excavations on Ofu Island. Ancient Samoan legends hold that the Manu'a Islands were the first to emerge at the command of the Samoan god Tagaloa. As a result, the kingly title of those islands, Tui Manu'a, accrued great authority, and the paramount chief of those islands held great sway throughout the region in pre-western contact days. In 1722 the Dutch explorer Jacob Roggeveen became the first Westerner to spy the Samoan Islands when he sighted the Manu'a Islands. Roggeveen was followed in 1768 by the French explorer Louis-Antoine de Bougainville who stopped at the Manu'a Islands and also sighted (but did not stop at) Tutuila. It was Bougainville who gave the islands their first western name when he called them the Navigator Islands because he was so impressed by the sailing skills of the indigenous inhabitants. The first explorer to stop at Tutuila was Jean-Francois de Galoup, Comte de la Perouse on his ill-fated Pacific exploration. Perouse stopped near Fagasa on the north coast of Tutuila where misunderstandings led to a rapidly escalating conflict between the French crew and the indigenous population, resulting in the deaths of a dozen or so French sailors and some 39 Samoans. The battle site near today's Aasu is marked by a monument to the French dead erected by the Government of France. In 1839, the United States Exploring Expedition under the command of Lieutenant Charles Wilkes stopped at Tutuila and stayed for a while at Pago Pago, conducting surveys. There was little further American interest in the islands until after the Civil War when Pago Pago Harbour was considered as a possible coaling station for the US Navy. In 1872, a US naval officer, Commander Richard W. Meade, in command of the *USS Narragansett* stopped at Tutuila at the behest of the US minister to Hawaii, Henry A. Peirce, and concluded a treaty with the local *Matai* granting the United States the exclusive right to establish a coaling and naval station at Pago Pago bay. Although Meade had not been instructed by Washington to conclude a treaty his treaty with the Samoans was not repudiated by the US government, but neither was it ratified by the US Senate.

The seafaring skills of the Samoans prompted the French explorer Bougainville to name the islands the Navigator Islands

Although the Samoan islands were considered to be independent, if not quite civilized, by the Western powers in the nineteenth century imperialistic urges began to attract several Western powers interested in establishing a colony in the islands. In the decades between 1870 and 1890, increasing political instability in the Samoan archipelago, and ultimately a civil war by rival political factions, created the conditions for imperial powers to move against the independence of the local government. Soon warships from Britain, Germany, and the United States were visiting Samoan waters as the big powers manoeuvred to take over the islands.

A Samoan weapon of the type used in pre-colonial internecine warfare

To forestall the colonisation of the Samoan archipelago King Kalakaua of the independent Kingdom of Hawaii took the extraordinary step of outfitting and despatching to Samoa the first and only major warship of the Hawaiian Navy. His Hawaiian

Majesty's Ship (*HHMS*) *Kaimiloa* carried Hawaiian diplomats to Samoa who entered into treaty relations with the Samoan government in an effort to create a Hawaiian protectorate over the islands that would forestall white rule. The imperial powers looked askance at this effort by Hawaii, and the Germans were sufficiently put out by it that they informed the United States that Germany would declare war on Hawaii if Hawaii continued to interfere with German designs on Samoa. A crisis was averted by the combination of a cyclone, which destroyed, or damaged, the western warships in Samoa, and by a revolution in Honolulu that severely circumscribed the powers of the monarch. A new Hawaiian ministry led by the descendants of Christian missionaries took office in Honolulu and recalled the Hawaiian warship. The imperial powers thereafter established a joint protectorate over Samoa that lasted about ten years. It was during this period that the United States obtained title to land in Pago Pago Harbour for the establishment of the coaling and naval station that Commander Meade obtained the rights from the Tutuila *Matai* in 1872.

HHMS Kaimiloa firing a salute at Samoa, 1887

By the end of the century, circumstances made it imperative to finally resolve the issue of who would control Samoa and negotiations began in Berlin in 1899, resulting in an agreement that the islands would be partitioned between Imperial Germany and the United States of America, with Great Britain obtaining colonial compensations elsewhere in return for surrendering its rights.

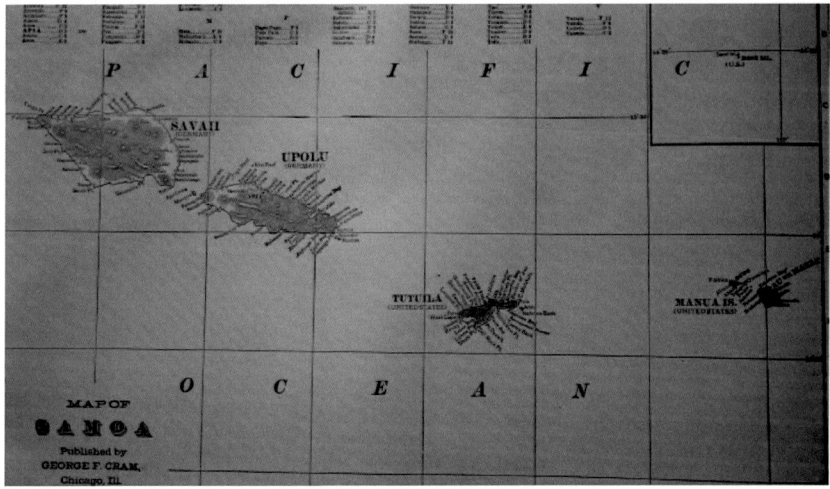

An early twentieth-century map showed the division of the Samoan archipelago between the United States and Imperial Germany

The following year, 1900, the United States formally proclaimed its sovereignty over the Samoan Islands of Tutuila and Aunu'u, upon receiving a deed of cession from the *Matai* of those islands. The *Matai* of the Manu'a Islands did not formally provide a deed of cession to the United States for those islands until 1904. Despite the early date of the cessions by the *Matai*, the US Congress did not ratify the cessions of the islands until 1929. After the commencement of US sovereignty in 1900, the islands were formally known as the US Naval Station Tutuila until 1911, when President William Howard Taft proclaimed that they should be known as American Samoa.

As the first naval commandant and *de facto* Governor following the partition Naval Commander Benjamin F. Tilley adopted a light-touch approach to colonial government. Perhaps he was influenced by what had happened in Hawaii when white settlers became dominant and the native Hawaiians subsequently lost their country. Tilley banned the sale of land to outsiders, thus ensuring that the indigenous population of American Samoa would not lose control of their lands as had happened in Hawaii following the *Great Mahele* of 1848. As a result, today much of the land in American Samoa continues to be communally owned. Tilley also left in place the local government structure based on the *aiga* and the village *Fono*, all under the supervision of the *Matai*. Tilley did proclaim that American law would apply in the islands but he also stipulated that traditional Samoan law would continue to apply where it did not conflict with American law. These sensible steps to protect the interests of the indigenous population were continued by Tilley's successors and they went a long way to preserve the interests and culture of the indigenous Samoans in American Samoa.

Commander Tilley recognized that the new territory would require some type of land force at least for internal order, if not also for external defence. Therefore, he sought and obtained permission from the US Navy Department for the enlistment of local Samoan men as US Navy Landsmen. That was the start of the *Fita Fita Guard*, with an original complement of 58 that was later expanded to 100 men. The *Fita Fita Guard* was seen as an elite military unit by American Samoans and considerable status accrued to its members in indigenous society. Many enlistees made the *Fita Fita Guard* their lifelong careers. The guard served on the local station ship, on small boats, and as radiomen. On land, they were guards and orderlies. They also formed a military band that held concerts on the *Malae*, or parade ground within the naval station at Pago Pago.

The American naval governors maintained cordial relations with their German counterparts in neighbouring German Samoa during the pre-war years, receiving formal visits from the German Governor of Samoa, and relations between the indigenous communities in the two colonies continued unabated. When World War One broke out in 1914, President Woodrow Wilson declared American neutrality in the war, and therefore the United States Navy at Pago Pago did not participate in the 1914 invasion and conquest of German Samoa by New Zealand forces.

In 1917 the United States entered the war on the side of the Entente and Allied powers (Britain, France, Russia, Italy, and Japan) and against the Central Powers (Germany, Austro-Hungary, and the Ottoman Empire). At the outset of the war two German merchant ships, the *Staatssekretar Solf* and the *Elsass* had sought refuge in neutral American Samoa where they had been interned by the US naval authorities. But once the US declared war on Germany the two ships were seized by the navy and their crews were imprisoned before being transferred to Hawaii.

The wooden steamer *Staatssekretar Solf* of 350 tons was built in 1913 by Stocks & Kolbe, shipbuilders of Kiel, Germany, for passenger and cargo transport between the islands of German Samoa. After its seizure by the US Navy, the naval authorities decided to convert the steamer into a gunboat for local defence, even though the ship's condition had deteriorated somewhat during its internment.

Dampfer „Staatsfekretär Solf".

The German Steamer *Staatssekretar Solf*, later the *USS Samoa* at her launch in 1914.

On June 12, 1917, by Executive Order 2635 President Wilson ordered that the title to the *Staatssekretar Solf* be vested in the United States and that the US Navy take over the ship for naval purposes. The ship was commissioned into the United States Navy as the *USS Samoa* on September 17, 1917. Thereafter the *USS*

Samoa, under the command of Lieutenant William T. Mallison, remained at Tutuila as a component of the US Asiatic Fleet. The 15,000-ton *Elsass* was towed to Hawaii by the navy.

In the late stages of the war, there was little threat to American Samoa. However, the Imperial German Navy was still active in Pacific waters late in the war in the form of a ship-rigged sailing vessel, SMS *Seeadler*, a German auxiliary cruiser operating as a raider in the southeastern Pacific. Under the command of Count Felix von Luckner, *Seeadler* took 16 prizes off South America and in the southeast Pacific before being wrecked on Mopelia Atoll in the Society Islands. *Seeadler's* crew (7 officers and 61 men) and her prisoners of war (30 men) were saved and von Luckner rigged a longboat as a sloop and armed it with small arms intending to reach Fiji with a small crew where he hoped to steal another sailing ship. Von Luckner was caught by the British authorities in Fiji before he could bring his plan to fruition. Meanwhile, back on Mopelia his remaining crew had managed to seize the French schooner *Lutece* in which they sailed to Easter Island where the Chilean authorities interned them. Back on Mopelia among the remaining shipwrecked prisoners of war a certain Captain Smith took charge of the *Seeadler's* remaining boat and sailed it with three American sailors to Pago Pago, where the US Navy made arrangements with the French authorities in Tahiti to rescue the remaining shipwrecked men at Mopelia.

SMS Seeadler circa 1916

To defend Pago Pago Harbour from the German raider threat the government ordered that one three-pounder gun and one 3-inch field artillery piece be positioned on Blunts Point and manned by ratings and officers from the naval station. The naval station facilities were closely guarded by naval ratings and the *Fita Fita Guard* on a twenty-four-hour basis. However, there were no attacks on American Samoa by German or Austo-Hungarian forces during the war.

The USS *Samoa* continued to make local cruises during the war, sailing west to Apia in occupied German Samoa and east to the Manu'a Islands, without incident. In 1920, after the end of the war, the *Samoa* was decommissioned and sold to a local shipping firm in Tutuila. It remains the only warship of the United States Navy to have borne the name *Samoa*.

After the war, America Samoa continued as a quiet naval backwater. German Samoa was now Western Samoa, a trust territory granted to benign New Zealand, which presented no security threats to the United States. Pago Pago became an itinerant diplomatic stop for New Zealand, British, and Australian officials, occasional French officials, and US congressional delegations.

The situation became very different when World War Two erupted in 1939. President Franklin Roosevelt declared American neutrality in the war but as time passed a growing antagonism developed between the Axis Powers (Japan, Germany, and Italy) and the United States and it was only a matter of time before events forced the United States to enter the war. War preparations in American Samoa began as early as February 1941, when President Roosevelt issued an Executive Order making Rose Atoll part of the Naval Defence Area, and the Navy ordered an anti-torpedo net installed across the opening of Pago Pago Harbour. In July 1941, the First Samoa Battalion, US Marine Corps Reserve was formed on Tutuila as the first ethnic unit to be incorporated into the US Marine Corps Reserves.

The war came to the United States on December 7, 1941. On that date, the Japanese Empire launched a massive assault on the Western powers with the intent of creating its Greater Asian Co-Prosperity Sphere, essentially a hegemonic empire across the Asia-Pacific region. The assault began with the surprise attack on the US Pacific Fleet at Pearl Harbour in Hawaii, which resulted in the destruction, or damage, of all of America's Pacific battleships. Fortunately, the three aircraft carriers assigned to the fleet were absent from Pearl Harbour and they would subsequently form the backbone of the US Navy's response to the attack. On the same day, Japanese forces bombed targets in the US-owned Philippines, preparatory to an invasion that soon came to those islands. In the ensuing days, the Japanese attacked other Pacific possessions of the United States, bombing Howland and Baker Islands killing two colonists, and bombing Wake Island. Both Howland Island and Jarvis Island were subsequently bombarded with shellfire from Japanese submarines. British Commonwealth and Dutch territories in the Pacific and Asian mainland were also assaulted by the Japanese Empire.

Immediately, President Roosevelt began assembling vast resources of materiel and manpower to extinguish the Axis threat and in the Pacific War, Pago Pago became the most important base for the support of US operations in the south-west Pacific war theatre. Some 30,000 US soldiers and marines would pass through Tutuila during the war on their way to the battlefields further to the west. Pago Pago became the headquarters of the Samoa Defence Group under the command of Marine General Henry Larsen, and by the summer of 1944, it included not only the entire Samoan Archipelago but had been also extended to include US bases on Bora Bora in the French-owned Society Islands, Aitutaki and Penrhyn in New Zealand's Cook Islands, Britain's Ellice Islands group, and the French Islands of Wallis and Futuna.

Although Japan did not invade American Samoa, the Imperial Japanese Navy made one attack upon it during the war. On January 11, 1942, a Japanese submarine surfaced off the north coast of Tutuila and opened fire on the Greater Pago Pago urban area with a 5.5-inch deck gun. The submarine fired 15 shells over ten minutes causing little damage and minor injuries to one civilian and one member of the *Fita Fita Guard*. Only four shells hit targets on land while all the rest of the shells fell into the harbour, where they did no damage. There was no return fire from the garrison forces probably owing to the concealment of the submarine behind the island's mountains. It was the only attack made by Japan on American Samoa in World War Two, although Japanese submarines continued to cruise through American Samoan waters throughout the war.

To forestall an invasion of Tutuila numerous concrete pillboxes were built along the coastline of the island as a first line of defence if an invasion did occur. Many of the World War Two era pillboxes still line the coast and we saw several of them on our road trips around the island. To defend the harbour at Pago Pago the navy installed four 6-inch coastal naval guns manufactured in 1907, two at Blunt's Point on the west side of Pago Pago Harbour, and two more at Breakers Point on the east side of the harbour. All four guns are still in place today and can be hiked to (although the Breakers Point Trail was closed when we visited). When they were operational, the guns had a range of 14.5 kilometres. A major airfield was completed at Tafuna on Tutuila Island in April 1942, most of which now forms part of the Pago Pago International Airport.

An abandoned World War II pillbox on the coast of Tutuila

By the middle of 1944, allied advances had backfooted the Japanese and it seemed certain that the war would eventually end with an Allied victory. Therefore, the First Samoan Battalion of the US Marines Reserves was stood down. Victory over Japan came in August 1945, after the defeats of Germany and Italy, and followed the US decision to drop atomic bombs on Hiroshima and Nagasaki in Japan.

After the war, the US demobilized and it soon became apparent that the large military installations in American Samoa would not be needed in peacetime. Following two world wars Germany and Japan were no longer a Pacific threat, and the remaining security issues lay along the Asia-Pacific littoral where the US had stationed military forces in Japan, Korea, and the Philippines. On December 31, 1949, the United States Naval Station Tutuila was demobilized and removed from the list of US Naval Establishments.

The presence of a US Naval Governor in American Samoa was now an anachronism, particularly as a post-war wave of decolonization began to swell, and as the Europeans began to give up their empires. In American Samoa, a transition began in 1948, when a local parliament, the American Samoa *Fono* was established, and a form of limited democracy began to function in the country. In 1951, the responsibility for the executive governance of American Samoa by the United States was transferred from the Navy Department to the Department of the Interior, and the last US Naval Governor turned over his office to a civilian Governor appointed by the Secretary of the Interior. The *Fita Fita Guard* was disbanded and those members of the guard who wished to remain with the US forces were allowed to transfer to Hawaii. Most of the members of the *Fita Fita Guard* and their families decamped Samoa for Hawaii which became the first large-scale migration of American Samoans out of their country. On July 1, 1951, the US Navy transferred the title to all of its property at the former US Naval Station Tutuila to the US Department of the Interior. After more than half a century of involvement in the affairs of American Samoa, the US Navy exited the country.

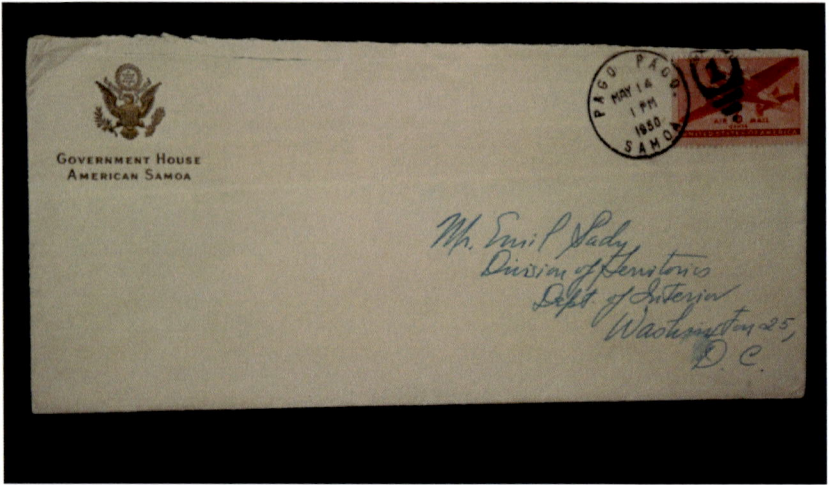

Postal History: A postal cover from Government House in the last days of the US naval governors

Throughout the 1950s a succession of civilian governors responsible to the Department of the Interior continued the US colonial administration of the country, albeit with the assistance now of a local parliament in the form of the *Fono*. Nevertheless, American Samoa languished as a backwater and there was barely any development in the country, despite the appointment of an American Samoan lawyer, Peter Tali Coleman, as the first indigenous governor of American Samoa in 1956. But after 1960, decolonization swept the globe, and colonial powers that were failing to develop their dependencies to assume self-government began to be criticized at the United Nations. The failures of the USA in American Samoa were highlighted in an expose by an American writer, Clarence Hall, in 1961, shortly after the activist administration of President John F. Kennedy took office in Washington. Hall compared the lack of development in American Samoa to a slum, and he suggested that it was a major embarrassment for the United States. Western countries and the communist bloc were locked in a struggle to influence the lesser developed countries and President Kennedy was trying to woo newly independent countries to support the United States. Consequently, it became imperative for the image of the United States for the Kennedy Administration to improve the lives of the residents of American Samoa, and President Kennedy flooded the islands with money and resources. There was a major upgrading of the infrastructure throughout American Samoa, and the island residents' standard of living rose accordingly. In 1962 New Zealand withdrew from Western Samoa, which became the first colonized Pacific island state to regain its independence from a Western power, setting an example for other Pacific islands.

By the Seventies, decolonization was reaching a fever pitch in the Pacific. Britain granted independence to Fiji, Tonga, the Gilbert Islands, the Ellice Islands, the Solomon Islands, and, together with France, the New Hebrides Islands. The United States returned the Ryukyu, Bonin, and Volcano Islands to Japan and began preparing the Caroline, Marshall, and Palau Islands in the US Trust Territory of the Pacific Islands for formal independence. Closer to American Samoa, the Cook Islands became an autonomous associated state of New Zealand with internal self-government. Given all of those changes, it was apparent that a further evolution of the political structure of American Samoa was desirable and necessary.

American Samoans had their own parliament since 1948 but the highest executive office had remained an appointed office in the gift of the US Secretary of the Interior and for a time American Samoans did express reluctance to any change in the executive office of the Territorial Government. However, in the mid-seventies that changed, and the direct election of a Territorial Governor and Lieutenant Governor was approved by the population in a referendum. The first election for the office of Governor was held in November 1977, and the first elected Governor, Peter Tali Coleman, took office in January 1978. Since that time all Governors and Lieutenant Governors of American Samoa have been members of the indigenous population. Thus, the change to an elected executive completed the process of vesting internal autonomy to

American Samoa, and government within the islands since then is now firmly in the hands of the indigenous population. The United States government retains constitutional paramountcy over the American Samoan government and it can continue to legislate about matters concerning American Samoa, although generally, it does not do so. The US Federal Government focuses its responsibilities relating to American Samoa on foreign relations, defence, fisheries management, and spending programs. A large part of the national income in American Samoa consists of US Federal grants.

In recent decades American Samoa has been beset by natural disasters that caused loss of life as well as economic losses. American Samoa is prone to cyclones and Cyclone Val, in 1991, was particularly damaging, destroying about 65% of the housing, and about 80% of the agricultural products. An even greater impact was caused by an underwater earthquake 190 kilometres south of Tutuila in 2009, registering 8.3 on the Richter scale and resulting in a tsunami that hit Tutuila with great force, causing significant damage. Thirty-four people in American Samoa were killed by the 2009 tsunami. During the COVID-19 Pandemic, American Samoa took extraordinary measures to prevent infected people from entering the country and spreading the disease but despite those precautions cases emerged there by the autumn of 2020, and eventually there was a total of more than 8000 cases during the Pandemic, with 34 known deaths.

7

Central Tutuila

Tutuila is the main island in the American Samoan group and it is the political and economic centre of the country. Almost all of our time was spent just on this island. Although we visited during the wet season, we enjoyed pleasant weather for the most part with the sun shielded by clouds only occasionally. As for rain, that fell mostly at night so for the most part we enjoyed pleasant days.

I had arranged for a rental car from Avis Rent a Car before travelling to American Samoa and, after a quick tour of the hotel and its environs in the morning following our arrival in the country, I waited in the lobby of the Tradewinds for a meeting with a woman from Avis who had promised to bring me my prearranged vehicle. I had anticipated an SUV so I was surprised to find that she brought along a Toyota Tacoma pick-up truck but I soon grew to favour it in our explorations of the mountainous roads on this island.

Around Tafuna

Tafuna is the largest village on Tutuila and it is the economic centre of the island and therefore of the country. Tafuna is the location of several American mainland fast food outlets, sewing and fashion shops, grocery stores, and all the basic services that one expects and needs in modern life. It is also the only part of Tutuila where private land sales are permissible.

Exploring close to our hotel we wandered into a local florist shop where Vi purchased a few tropical silk flowers to wear in her hair and we chatted amiably with the ladies in charge of the store, complimenting them on their floral creations. Close by the florists was a Vietnamese restaurant and I enjoyed a bowl of *Pho* there, while my wife chatted with the charming young Vietnamese woman who served us. She told us that she had recently arrived in American Samoa to work but naturally, she was experiencing some pangs of homesickness. Farther afield we ventured into two local marketplaces, a KS Food store, which is a standard grocery store, and a Cost-U-Less store, which seemed to be the local version of a Costco bulk store. However, I was interested to learn later that the Cost-U-Less store was not affiliated with Costco but rather traces its origins to the storied Hudson Bay Company that is so closely entwined with the history of Canada.

There isn't very much to see in Tafuna from a tourism perspective but one feature that does exist here, and that I was anxious to see concerned the famous star mounds in American Samoa. In the ancient society of the Samoan Archipelago, star mounds were elevated platforms of up to three metres in height and roughly shaped like a star that were used by the *Matai* for pigeon snaring, a highly competitive activity practised by the elites of Samoan society. There is speculation that the star mounds were so important that they could reflect the amount of *mana*, or spiritual power, that an individual *Matai* possessed. They might also have been the scene of religious rituals in addition to pigeon snaring. In the Christian era on Tutuila, the use of the star mounds was suppressed and the Christian missionaries deprecated them as a source of paganism that was to be avoided by Christian believers. As a result, many of the star mounds deteriorated or were lost to the ravages of time. However, we learned that one of the best-preserved star mounds was in Tafuna, close to the Tradewinds Hotel, and so I resolved to see it.

Finding this particular star mound, which is called the *Tia Seu Lupe Star Mound* was not easy. The first time I tried to look for it I got lost in a maze of unnamed streets. During my second attempt, I made a point of asking the desk clerks at Tradewinds how to find it but I quickly noticed a certain reticence among them. Either they did not know where it was or they were reluctant to say where it was. Perhaps, I thought, there is still a lingering Christian taboo about such sites in contemporary Samoan culture. Nevertheless, I did eventually get directions to it from the female security person on duty and I was able to locate it without too much difficulty by following her directions. It was located quite near a statue of the Holy Mother erected on the grounds of the Roman Catholic Cathedral in Tafuna.

The site of the *Tia Seu Lupe Star Mound* in Tafuna

A wooden viewing platform that once afforded good viewing access to the site has now fallen. Dense vegetation has overgrown the mound so it is somewhat difficult to obtain a clear idea of its dimensions and its two-tiered features. A restoration project is currently in the planning stage. A monument on the site of the viewing platform does provide some information about *Tia* (mounds) and describes them as scattered about on the Tafuna plain, often on the tops of ridges. Mostly star-shaped, *Tia* have anywhere from one to eleven arms, with eight arms being the most common form of construction. In ancient times the star mounds were actively used during the southern hemisphere winter. Somewhat to my surprise, the description of the Tafuna *Tia Seu Lupe Star Mound* described it as having a somewhat different physical structure than most other star mounds in American Samoa but without actually saying what that difference was!

Similar to our visits to various *heiau* in Hawaii and in French Polynesia, the Tafuna *Tia Seu Lupe* was a quiet and now forgotten reminder to us of the ancient cultures of the South Seas that have passed out of human memory, following the collision of those ancient cultures with western civilization.

The Greater Pago Pago Urban Area

Having explored Tafuna somewhat we next turned our sights on Pago Pago, the nearby territorial capital. After wending our way through a series of local roads we embarked on Route 001, the main coastal highway on Tutuila. Route 001 is not the sort of highway that a North American would expect. The speed limit on Tutuila is a maximum of 40 kilometres per hour (25 miles per hour) and is sometimes less than that. Speed restrictions are largely obeyed and are certainly enforced. On this island, life slows down. Inland on Route 001 heading east towards Pago Pago we passed several commercial establishments including merchandise stores, restaurants, and a gas station. A few of them stood out to us. There was a movie theatre, the only one on the island, running recently released movies sent out from the US mainland. We spied a dress shop called Happy Fashions, whose store windows were filled with the petite white mannequins one frequently sees in North American store windows but which looked totally out of place here where the local population tended towards the robust, being generally larger in stature than their North American equivalents. There was also a funerary shop that displayed caskets for sale in the store's front windows, which is something one would probably never see in North America, where any matters linked to death are carefully tucked away out of sight.

Soon the road reached the South Pacific coast and the magnificent harbour of Pago Pago, one of the most spectacular natural harbours in the world, opened before us. This was the harbour that drove American interest in acquiring these islands in the late nineteenth century and it is easy to see why. The Pago Pago Harbour makes for an excellent protected harbour for ships and is expansive enough to support large naval forces. Coastal Route 001 provided a beautiful drive into the capital of American Samoa. Along the way we watched blue Pacific rollers reaching for the island and we passed the famous Flowerpot Island, also known as *Fatu* Rock, and its smaller shoreside neighbour *Futi* Rock. These two natural features commemorate a famous legend about two lovers who were forced to leave their homes in Samoa because their families would not agree to their union. Their canoe sank off Tutuila and the ocean swallowed them but because of their love they were transformed into these two offshore features and the nearby village is called Fatumafuti in their honour. Today, the small Flowerpot island is covered in lush vegetation and hosts a multitude of birds and native bats.

Fatu or Flowerpot Rock

What is geographically described as the municipality of Pago Pago is, in reality, several independent villages linked together along the shoreline of Pago Pago Harbour and forming a larger urban area. Each section of this urban area consists of separately named villages within this whole urban area (and Pago Pago itself is merely one of these villages, though giving its name to the larger area).

Throughout the island, there is a system of private colourful buses called *aiga* buses that all pass through the Greater Pago Pago urban area on their way to the remoter reaches of the island. The buses are converted trucks and are painted in many different colours and designs by their owners. They are a colourful conveyance on the island.

Within the Greater Pago Pago urban area, several sites can attract the attention of visitors and we looked forward to exploring this area. Our first stop for exploration brought us to an important point in American Samoa's World War II history - the Blunt's Point Trail and Battery.

Blunt's Point Trail and Battery

The Blunt's Point Trail, officially a part of the National Park of American Samoa, is a rather rough and rocky trail that starts in the village of Gataivai and goes for about 0.8 of a kilometre, winding its way up to two 6-inch gun emplacements built by the US military to defend Pago Pago Harbour during World War II. The coastal guns are still in place though they are no longer useable. At first, we started going the wrong way on the trail but nearby construction workers shouted out to us and told us which way to go. As we went up the trail, we happened to flush out a few of the ubiquitous feral chickens on the island who complained loudly about our presence. It is a fairly steep ascent up this trail, though manageable, and the trail passes an old abandoned ammunition magazine before the trail reaches the gun emplacement. There is a round cement gun mount on which the six-inch gun sits pointing out to a sea from which no enemy has appeared in many decades. The gun emplacement was constructed to afford the gunners a wide range in which to target any enemy vessels seeking to attack the harbour.

One of two massive naval coastal guns at Blunt's Point

The Jean P. Haydon Museum

Our next stop in the Pago Pago area was at the Jean P. Haydon Museum, established by a former American Governor of the territory in memory of his wife. We were now in the village of Fagatogo, which is the administrative sector of the country and most of the public and national institutions are located in this village. Years ago many American Samoan artifacts were located at Government House and it was Governor Haydon who was moved to establish a national museum for American Samoa and to transfer the Government House artifacts to the new museum.

When we entered the building there were a couple of men sitting at a table who mentioned to us that the museum and its contents were under renovation but that we were free to look around the museum. In its current state, we found the museum to be more of a warehouse of artifacts than a true museum. There was an absence of true curation and little in the way of contextual information. Still, the artifacts provided a sense of the Samoan culture prevalent in the islands and there were some interesting things to see. We thought that this could become a very interesting museum in the future with the right approach to curation and artifact display. Since it was said to be under renovation, it may well become a much more informative exposition of the local history and culture. For us, at the time of our visit, I am afraid that it was a bit of a disappointment.

A collection of artifacts at the Haydon Museum

Tauese P.F. Sunia Ocean Centre

Far more inviting and informative was our visit to the Tauese P. F. Sunia Ocean Centre, a facility associated with the US National Oceanic and Atmospheric Administration (NOAA) which described itself in a brochure that I collected at this Centre as "the most important agency you've never heard of." In addition to the Ocean Centre, the NOAA has a sampling station on Tutuila that samples the quality of the air. NOAA was said to have determined that Tutuila has the purest air quality in the South Pacific, and perhaps in the world.

The Ocean Centre serves as the visitor centre for the National Marine Sanctuary of American Samoa, a vast marine protected area within the territory of American Samoa. The Centre consists of a large space devoted to explaining the ecosystems of the oceans and the crucial importance of the coral reefs that surround the Pacific islands, including those within American Samoa. The threats of pollution and global warming to the oceanic environment are explored, and there are links to the importance of the seas to Samoan culture.

Within American Samoan territory six areas have been set aside as marine sanctuaries of the United States encompassing 35,174 square kilometres of coral reefs and open ocean. Three of the marine sanctuaries are located on Tutuila at Fagatele Bay, Fagalua, and Fogama'a Coves, and also at Aunu'u Island, a small neighbouring island to Tutuila. All of the protected areas on Tutuila or Aunu'u islands are accessible to locals and visitors who wish to explore them by snorkel or scuba. The other three protected areas are much more remote, located on the southern shore of Ta'u Island, on Rose Atoll, and on Swains Island.

Displays at the Tauese P.F. Sunia Ocean Centre

The rotunda, which is the main display room in the Sunia Centre, holds static displays on the ocean environment as well as a large two-metre diameter sphere that is suspended from the ceiling and portrays the Earth but it can also display videos and dynamic information. The friendly staff member who was in charge of the Centre when we visited set up the sphere to show us videos about the marine sanctuary and a current picture of air traffic over North America. A smaller room contained exhibits specific to each of the protected sanctuaries in American Samoa, and information on the particular species of marine life that are likely to be encountered within territorial waters. We learned some very interesting things about the underwater world of American Samoa, as well as the important role that it plays in the local culture of the islands.

The Sunia Ocean Centre showcases the National Marine Sanctuary of American Samoa

The *Fono*

Ambling further along on the main road in the Greater Pago Pago urban district while remaining in Fagatogo, we came across the *Fono* or parliament of American Samoa. The location of the *Fono* was a substantial construction site because the former structure, which had been designed to capture the architectural style of a Samoan *fale*, had been demolished and a new larger concrete structure was rising in its place, still following, in a general way a *fale* design. The House of Representatives, the lower house of the American Samoan parliament was meeting elsewhere as a consequence but an adjacent building identified itself as the Senate of American Samoa and so I ventured inside to inquire if we might have a look at the Senate Chamber. Vi looked askance at this effort of mine, thinking that it was intrusive, but actually, the charming young woman who met us at the reception desk was very welcoming and she readily agreed to give us a tour. She explained that the Senate of American Samoa was not a popularly elected body. Rather, the Senators were appointed to a term of four years by the *Matai*, the Chiefs and High Chiefs of American Samoa, who continue to hold sway in the villages. The purpose of this arrangement is to ensure that the cultural integrity of American Samoan society cannot be undermined by political pressures emanating from the lower house, which is a popularly elected assembly. We found that constitutional design to be familiar because in our country the upper house of the Parliament (which is also called the Senate) is appointed rather than elected, a mechanism originally designed to protect regional interests from initiatives arising in the popularly elected lower house.

Our guide led us first into the preliminary chamber where two long banks of tables and chairs were set up facing each other and our guide explained that it is customary in the American Samoan Senate for Senators to meet and dine informally in this chamber before the convening of a session in the formal Senate Chamber. It seems that this charming procedure reinforces collegiality among the members, and it contributes to better outcomes in the Senate Chamber.

We then walked through into the main white-columned Senate Chamber, where two facing rows of desks and chairs were placed on a hardwood floor. The facing rows are mediated by the Senate Speaker's chair and podium, which is placed at the head of the Chamber, and which is flanked by blue curtains and the flags of the United States and American Samoa. In front of the Speaker's chair was a block of wood with the inscription *Maota Maualuga, Amerika Samoa*, which, roughly translated, means Upper House of American Samoa.

Above us, the upper part of the Chamber was wood-panelled and upon it were displayed the portraits of the current Senators. The high-ceiling roof of the Senate Chamber was of traditional construction.

The Senate Chamber of the *Fono* in American Samoa

Our well-informed guide explained that for the most part, the relations among American Samoan Senators are cordial and collegial, and without overt partisanship. Politics in the territory does follow the forms of American politics so there is a division between adherents of the Democratic Party and adherents of the Republican Party. However, the Democratic Party has far more supporters than the Republican Party in American Samoa, and that is reflected in the composition of the Senate which primarily consists of Democrats. Most of the Governors who have been popularly elected have also been Democrats, although there has been one independent Governor.

Appointments to the Senate are the preserve of the *Matai* and Senators are selected through a consensus process, with various *Matai* taking turns serving as Senators almost on a rotational basis. Our guide was particularly pleased to point out to us the portrait of the only female Senator, who is currently serving in an otherwise overwhelmingly male body. The female Senator is herself a high chief, holding a title that once belonged to her father. There is also one female Representative in the House of Representatives of American Samoa and the non-voting Congressional Representative of American Samoa in Washington, D.C., is an American Samoan woman so there is room for an expansion of female representation. Our guide looked forward to the day when more women might obtain legislative offices in American Samoa.

As we left the American Samoan Senate, expressing our gratitude for a very informative tour to our guide she gave us a special pin as a memento of our visit. The striking silver and black pin commemorated, in 2023, the 75th anniversary of the establishment of the American Samoan *Fono* in 1948.

A pin commemorating the 75th anniversary of the *Fono*

The Fagatogo Market

Continuing our explorations of the urban centre of American Samoa, we next came upon the Fagatogo Market. This outdoor market is the place to stop for fresh produce from local producers. Vi always loves these outdoor markets so there was no question that we were going to stop as we passed by. The Fagatogo Market is the major outdoor market in the Greater Pago Pago urban area. Residents come here to satisfy their demand for local fresh fruits and vegetables including coconuts, breadfruit, taro, and bananas, among others. The interior of the marketplace also hosts vendors selling tee shirts, summer dresses, and other items. We stopped to purchase some bananas before moving on.

Produce at the Fagatogo Market

The US Naval Station Tutuila Historic District

Still in Fagatogo, we now found ourselves in the heart of what once was the US naval establishment at Pago Pago - the Historic Naval District. Before coming to American Samoa I had obtained a brochure published by the American Samoa Historic Preservation Office entitled "A Walking Tour of Historic Fagatogo." The Fagatogo district at Pago Pago was once the site of the US Naval Station Tutuila and many of its buildings have now been repurposed for public administration. Originally, the naval officers and ratings assigned to the Pago Pago station were billeted aboard their ships in the harbour but the navy began erecting buildings in 1902, and by the end of the US Naval administration in 1951, the naval station encompassed 87 hectares with 105 buildings or other structures. Today, only eleven naval structures remain within Fagatogo and the neighbouring Utulei district of Greater Pago Pago, and those structures are listed for protection on the US

National Register of Historic Places as the US Naval Station Tutuila Historic District.

We had already visited one of those historic buildings – the Jean P. Haydon Museum, which was constructed in 1919, and at one time served as the Commissary Building for the US Naval Station. Today the museum building also incorporates a smaller structure in the rear that was originally a naval garage, with a possibly earlier construction date than the main part of the museum. The next building on our path was the Office of the Territorial Registrar, which was formerly the Radio Station for the US Navy. At one time large radio masts were erected behind this building.

Across the street was the *Malae*, a large grass field used for ceremonies, such as the annual Flag Day celebration of American annexation. The *Malae* in the naval historic district is formally called the *Malae o le Talu* but in the days when the US Navy ruled here this grass field was the Naval Parade Ground. This is where the *Fita Fita Guard* and Band once drilled and practised.

Close by was the *Fita Fita* Barracks, which was constructed in 1908 by the members of the *Fita Fita Guard*, the local auxiliary of the US Navy. A huge feast marked the dedication of the barracks in 1908, but today the *Fita Fita Guard* is long gone and what was once their barracks is now the headquarters of the American Samoa Department of Public Safety. Close by is the former Samoan Jail, which was also under naval jurisdiction and once held the German prisoners of war who were taken from the interned German merchant ships in World War One after the USA entered the war.

The former Fita Fita Barracks in the Naval Historic District

In addition to a couple of vintage churches that are within the naval historic district the US Naval Station Tutuila Historic District also includes Government House high on Observatory Point and the former Naval Administration Building, which has now been re-purposed as the High Court of American Samoa. That building was originally constructed in 1904 and restored in 1998 to look as closely as possible to the way it looked at the time of its construction. Not only the exterior of the building is historically authentic — great care was taken to ensure that the interior was also preserved and restored. I wanted to see the interior, as the publication from the American Samoa Historic Preservation Office stated: "The Court House interior deserves a visit — much of the original interior woodwork was also preserved and restored, including the central staircase and skylight."

The former Naval Administration Building, now the High Court of Justice of America Samoa

Being a lawyer myself by profession I had just assumed that the courthouse would be open to the public. Well, not so in American Samoa! When we entered we immediately walked through a metal detector and were met by two gentlemen, one of whom politely asked us what case we were there for. I explained that we were not participating in a case but that we were visitors and we wanted to see the interior of the courthouse. Consternation! Apparently, in American Samoa, you cannot just enter a courthouse without a legal purpose. Only litigants, their witnesses, and their attorneys are permitted to enter.

Despite being unwanted I saw that I was standing next to an empty courtroom so I bargained a little with the two gentlemen and they agreed to at least let us peek into an empty courtroom provided that I promised not to take any photographs. So we were able to see the restored original interior woodwork, which was a nicely stained dark colour Dutch Lap, but unfortunately, we were unable to get a glimpse of the other architectural elements mentioned in the guidebook. Meanwhile, Vi was mortified by the whole episode and so I had to forgo any further exploration of the historic district.

8

The Coastal Road East

On another day we explored the countryside of Tutuila. We drove through all of metropolitan Pago Pago and along the gritty east side of the harbour, past the Ronald Reagan shipyard and then the Star-Kist Tuna Fish Plant, which is the largest private sector employer on Tutuila, second only to the government as a major employer.

People of a certain vintage, like myself, will have fond memories of the Star Kist cartoon mascot, Charlie the Tuna, who appeared in the 1960s and 1970s television commercials extolling the quality of the Star-Kist tuna products. Charlie's perennial attempts to be selected by Star-Kist fishers were always unsuccessful since he was never deemed to be quite good enough for the company. A statue of Charlie has been placed on the grounds of the Star-Kist Plant in Pago Pago.

Soon we turned due south at Aua and later east towards the far eastern end of Tutuila. Away from the urban centres we found a more tranquil setting as we passed small villages along a beautiful coastline, stopping occasionally to take photos. We stopped to photograph an old coastal pillbox from World War II that would have served to protect the island if a Japanese invasion force had ventured this far east during the war. We also spied a United States Coast Guard cutter putting out to sea from Pago Pago Harbour. In American Samoa, the US Coast Guard provides marine law enforcement, homeland security in territorial waters, fishery patrols to prevent illegal fishing, and promotes nautical safety.

A US Coast Guard Cutter slips out of Pago Pago Harbour in the early morning

Away from the urban area and meandering through the small villages along the coast one could almost imagine a simpler time before Samoa's collision with the West when the patterns of life might have followed the idyllic routines of a state of nature. But idyllic times were now long past even in this somewhat isolated paradise and all of the intrusions of modern life from mini-marts to television, to cell phones, and the internet are present in even the smallest villages. Housing is no longer the thatched open *fales* of former times but is now well-maintained concrete or concrete block homes. Still, if Tutuila was no longer in a state of nature, it remained a beautiful place as we remarked to ourselves while continuing to drive along Route 001 to the eastern end of the island. Beautiful beaches beckoned to us but we resisted the temptations for the moment.

A scene along the eastern coastline

Along the Coast

Our destination was the ferry dock for the small ferries to Aunu'u

Island, Tutuila's small neighbour to the southeast. We saw Aunu'u between the twists and turns in the road as we drove east long before the road reached it. But we were so involved with our pretty surroundings that I actually missed the turn-off for the ferries and it was only when I realised that Aunu'u Island was now in my rear-view mirror that I realised that we had driven too far. So we turned around in the village of Alao on the eastern extremity of Tutuila and drove back to the village of Au'asi where we located the ferry slip.

Aunu'u Island

We parked in the small and crowded parking area on the landing and we walked up to the pavilion that overlooked the sheltered ferry dock where the small ferries would make land. There were no ferries currently in port so we settled ourselves down to wait. There was only one other person present when we arrived, a young woman who was speaking on her cell phone. Soon afterwards, we struck up a conversation with her and found her to be a friendly and delightful acquaintance, like so many of the people that we met on these islands. She was a 28-year-old school teacher who lived on Aunu'u Island but she taught at a school on Tutuila, so she was very familiar with the workings of the ferries and she explained how long we would wait for one, and the length, and costs, of a trip over to her island. Sure enough, I soon heard her say that a ferry was coming over. At first, I could not see anything but she pointed out where to look and then I spied a small boat making its way out of Aunu'u Island and heading towards Tutuila.

Our fellow passenger had several boxes with her and she explained that she had stayed over on Tutuila on Friday night because there was a staff appreciation party at the school where she worked, and she was now heading home with some provisions. She told us that she lived on Aunu'u with her family and that her father was the local pastor on the island. I asked about life on the island and she mentioned that the population was small, perhaps a couple of hundred people and she confirmed something else that I had heard about Aunu'u, which was that it is a very conservative island, even more conservative in its social mores than Tutuila.

Soon the ferry arrived, a small motorised catamaran-type vessel with crosswise bench-sitting and some additional benches along the gunwales. A few other people had joined us and we crowded aboard while the young men who crewed the boat stowed the boxes that our young acquaintance was taking home with her to Aunu'u. Once we were all aboard, the crew cast off and we started out of the small protected harbour towards our destination, which was about two kilometres away. Though small, the craft seemed quite safe and although we did not have to wear any life jackets I saw that there was a pile of life jackets stowed forward on the boat. However, the sea was calm, the sun was out, we were shaded on the boat, and the trip over to Aunu'u was a pleasant sea excursion that lasted about twenty minutes before we entered the protected harbour on the island and docked.

Looking towards Tutuila from Aunu'u Island

At the wharf we parted company with the young teacher who was our fellow traveller but not before she had offered Vi refreshments at her nearby home, having noted that we had a limited supply of water with us. Vi was very impressed by her hospitality and concern. It was another example of the quick offering of friendship that we experienced in American Samoa.

Before departing the young schoolteacher pointed us down the coastal road and invited us to explore her island. She also encouraged us to strike up a conversation with anyone we met along the way but as it turned out we met no one. As we walked along the coastal road, I noted that the authorities had created a rock wall along the waterside to prevent wave erosion. We passed a noisy generator that supplied electricity to the island. Among the scattered trees, I spotted a colourful Pacific Kingfisher.

The Coastal Road on Aunu'u Island

Geologically, Aunu'u is a product of volcanic activity and to geologists, it exhibits basalt rock with interleaving layers of tuff, a form of volcanic ash. The island is quite small - only about 150 hectares in area and it is covered in tropical vegetation except where the townsite and the taro patches exist. It is apparently the only place in the country where taro is grown in paddy fields. Aunu'u is also noteworthy because it hosts the only freshwater lake in American Samoa and it is reputed to have an area of red quicksand. These were all natural features that I wanted to see but regrettably, we had forgotten to bring sunscreen with us on this trip and the sun beat down upon us excruciatingly. There was no respite because the road we walked on was covered with white sand and it reflected the sun's rays back upon us. We walked as far as the road existed before it turned inwards as a dirt trail. Where the road turned there was a rocky beach and we stopped there to admire the work of water erosion on the rock face before turning back. Much of the offshore area of Aunu'u is protected as part of the Marine Sanctuary of American Samoa because there is a great deal of marine diversity at Aunu'u owing to the presence of both shallow and deep reefs.

Erosion along the rocky shore of Aunu'u Island

Back at the harbour, we rested while waiting for the next ferry.

The village was rather quiet - the perfect image of a sleepy South Seas setting. It does have one notable historical connection, however. During the 1880s, King Kalakaua of Hawaii attempted to forestall the colonisation of the Samoan islands by outfitting and despatching the island kingdom's only warship, *HHMS Kaimiloa*. Unfortunately, the Hawaiian warship was plagued by inefficiencies and ill-discipline. At a stop at Pago Pago, four cannons from the ship were traded for pigs and three of those cannons ended up mounted on Aunu'u, where a few of the Hawaiian sailors left the *Kaimiloa* and settled on the island, marrying local women. The cannons from the *Kaimiloa* were erected near the village as a defence during the politically chaotic and fraught period that preceded the partition of the Samoan Archipelago by Imperial Germany and the United States at the end of the nineteenth century. It seems that the cannons were used by the Aunu'u islanders, assisted by the Hawaiian sailors who settled on Aunu'u, to successfully repel a large canoe invasion of the island. Today, the *Kaimiloa's* cannons are part of the collection of the Haydon Museum in Pago Pago.

The ferry dock at the small harbour on Aunu'u Island

We soon caught the ferry back to Tutuila and then we were on our way back to Pago Pago and Tafuna but along the way, we sought out a special place we had heard much about earlier - Tisa's.

Tisa's Barefoot Bar and Eco Lodge

A celebrated locale on Tutuila is Tisa's Barefoot Bar and Eco Lodge. Multiple tourist guidebooks mentioned this establishment and recommended it as a place to stop and kick back for a while. We searched for it on our way back from our trip to Aunu'u Island and we found it alongside the road, heavily screened by the tropical vegetation. I turned off of the road opposite Tisa's onto a narrow parking lane on the landward side of the road next to more lush tropical vegetation. There was a traffic cone on the lane and I carefully manoeuvred my truck to avoid hitting it. While I was doing that another, seemingly identical, white pick-up truck pulled into the lane behind us and also parked. As I got out of my vehicle a booming female voice shouted out "You parked in my driveway!" Immediately chagrined that I had done something wrong I started offering my profuse apologies but the woman just laughed aloud and waived off my concerns saying "No - you parked just where we want you to." It was Tisa herself together with her partner, who goes by the name of Candyman. We had arrived right at the same time as Tisa and Candyman were returning from a personal trip. The Candyman explained that Tisa's was not yet open for food service but that we could order drinks if we wished, and Tisa said to us "Yes, come in," so in we went and located a table overlooking the beach, and the ocean.

Looking over the Ocean from Tisa's

Tisa's place consists of a rustic and weatherbeaten driftwood-style open bar and restaurant right on the shore of the ocean. To our left, as we sat were a couple of traditional-style thatch huts that visitors could rent if they wished to get a real sense of what South Seas living would have been like in pre-western contact days. Vi remarked to our hosts: "This is a very nice restaurant" to which Tisa responded in a voice full of emphasis, "This isn't a restaurant - It's a sanctuary!" Truly then, I realised that Tisa really was one of the larger-than-life characters on these islands.

The driftwood bar at Tisa's

The flag of American Samoa is proudly displayed at Tisa's

We ordered a couple of beers and we sat overlooking the South Pacific. The sanctuary, as Tisa called it, was otherwise empty and we had the place to ourselves. It was an enchanting place surrounded by lush vegetation lulled by the sounds of the sea and with all of the South Seas ambience of a driftwood bar that only we could possess for the moment. After a while, the temptation of the sea proved to be too much for me and I went down some vertical logs positioned in the sand as steps for a swim in the ocean. As Vi watched me from the deck above a large blue parrotfish swam languorously by in the water towards some rocks offshore.

Alegra Beach at Tisa's

Tisa's is located on Alega Beach, one of the beaches recommended for swimming in the tourist guidebooks and the waters were warm and inviting. I swam along in parallel to the beach and to Tisa's place, sometimes floating and looking upwards at the lush greenery of Tutuila. Eventually, our quiet interlude here at Tisa's had to end and so we found ourselves back on the road heading west back to Pago Pago and Tafuna.

9

The Coastal Road West

A Sunday in American Samoa found us back on Route No. 001 this time heading to the western end of the island and then shifting northwest to the end of the road. Sunday was a fine day for a drive along the coast because, in this intensely Christian society, almost everything else shuts down on a Sunday, except for the Churches. Sunday is truly the Lord's Day here and it is a social imperative for people to spend it in worship, and family gatherings. So, with most things, even many beaches, closed for the day, a road trip made eminent sense to us. And so we began our long drive on Route One to the western extremities of Tutuila.

As we drove along passing by community churches we could hear beautiful voices lifted up in song, as well as some of what we took to be old-style fire and brimstone preaching. When we came across churches where services had ended we beheld many residents out in their Sunday best clothes. Women and girls were usually dressed all in white, while the men dressed in dark trousers and wore white shirts. Many American Samoan residents generously donate money to their churches and it shows since the churches are always the best-maintained structures in the villages.

Well-maintained churches are ever-present in American Samoa

As in our previous road trips on Tutuila, the free-roaming dogs were ubiquitous and I had to take care to avoid them if they sought to cross the road near us and to also take care if we stopped and alighted because then they might congregate near our vehicle and not all American Samoan dogs are friendly.

Our drive along the coast on the west side of Tutuila was picturesque and we stopped along the way several times to take photographs. The vistas overlooking the coastal section of the road were beautiful, and the small villages that we passed through were quite charming.

A scene along the west coast

The western coastline

A quiet beach on a Sunday afternoon

A picturesque village along the west coastal road

Eventually, we reached the western end of Tutuila near Cape Taputapu and the road began to swing north and then northwest, rising sharply as it ventured into the mountains. As we ascended and turned north and northwest the rainforest closed in and we often felt as if we were travelling through a tunnel of green vegetation so dense were the plants and trees that surrounded us.

Given the isolation of the northwest, the road in this area was not constructed to quite the same standard as the coastal portion of Route 001, although it was still paved throughout. In some parts the road narrowed and sharp turns and switchbacks ensured that drivers had to pay close attention lest they encounter a mishap.

Lush forests cover the mountains as the road rises towards the Northwest coast

Beautiful ocean vistas await the traveller as the road rises into the mountains

Dense foliage prevails along the road in the northwest

The evening before there had been heavy rains in Tafuna and I imagined that those rains also extended to the far west of the island as well because the road in the northwest rising from Cape Taputapu was heavily strewn with broken vegetation, including all manner of branches and leaves from the tropical rainforest through which were passing. There were even coconuts on the road and I had to take evasive action several times to avoid hitting them. At one point a stream was overflowing across the roadway and I had to go slowly to cross the water spilling over the pavement. Eventually, after many more twists and turns in the mountains, the road descended towards the sea and we once again reached the coast at the end of the road in the quiet village of Fagamalo, where we stopped to take a few photos. Of course, we then had to retrace our path through the mountainous road once again crunching over the fallen leaves and branches and dodging the coconuts on the road. We continued on Route 001 back to Tafuna, still enjoying this picturesque drive.

The end of the Road at Fagamalo

10

The National Park of American Samoa

A part of American Samoa that we were determined not to miss during our visit was the National Park of American Samoa, the most far-flung and often said to be the least visited national park in the US system of national parks. This national park is also famous because it contains the only true paleo-tropical rainforest in the US national park system and it is also notable because the lands of the national park are not owned by the US government but are only leased by the US government from the communal landholders. The National Park of American Samoa includes within its boundaries about 5500 hectares of land and 910 hectares of offshore underwater area. The rainforest is similar to Old World rainforests and has many species of plants and trees that are found in Asia. The park also supports the principles of *Fa'a Samoa* and therefore, unlike other US National Parks, some agriculture in the form of subsistence farming is permitted within the park boundaries.

Before venturing into the park itself we sought out the National Park of American Samoa Visitor Centre in Pago Pago. There we met a lively young American Samoan woman named Mel who gave us a personal orientation to the displays in the park office as well as information about the trails and points of interest in the national park. Mel was born in American Samoa but she had lived a considerable portion of her childhood and youth in Illinois. As a result, she bridged two cultures, American Samoan culture and the national culture of the United States. She had returned to live on Tutuila around the time of a national disaster, the 2009 tsunami that inundated the coastal plains of American Samoa and caused severe losses of life, and substantial property damage. The island was hit particularly hard by the 2009 wave and at the time there was no living memory of tsunamis on Tutuila. Mel related that it was a very trying time to return and to readapt to island life because the people were traumatized by the tsunami disaster.

I was interested in how she had adjusted culturally to life in Tutuila after living such a large part of her life on the American mainland. Of course, she said, there were cultural adjustments that she had to make, even though, as a Samoan living in the United States, she possessed an understanding of *Fa'a Samoa*. Now, with her knowledge of both American mainland culture and American Samoan culture, she was able to assess the powerful impact of American culture on the island culture. Although the unique Samoan culture remained intact in Tutuila, she noted that some local traditions seemed to be diminishing in American Samoa.

One diminishing tradition that Mel pointed out was the custom of providing a finely woven mat, an *ie toga*, at important rights of passage such as marriage, a titling ceremony, or at a memorial to a deceased person. The skill (and patience) required to make the *ie toga* with its very fine or tight weave is increasingly hard to find in American Samoa because the specialized knowledge to make these mats is not being passed down to succeeding generations as much as it was in the past. Another woman that I spoke to on Tutuila also told us that the traditional art of making the *ie toga* was not as prevalent on the island as it once had been and that many people were compelled to acquire the traditional mats from the islands of Upolu or Savai'i, in neighbouring Samoa whenever they are required for ceremonies in American Samoa.

As a result, Mel informed us that she was contemplating creating a program at the National Park for American Samoan youth to teach them this traditional skill. She said that she was able to consider doing this because one of her co-workers at the National Park Office possessed the skill set that was necessary to make an *ie toga*. Through such a program the US National Park Service may be able to help to preserve the ways of *Fa'a Samoa* for a new generation.

A Siapo and an ie toga at the National Park Office

Mel also gave us some tips on the trail system in the National Park and cautioned us that while we could access the trails within the National Park on Sundays it was preferable to hike on another day owing to the local practice of keeping the Sabbath as a holy day and as a day of rest. Before leaving the park office we obtained two of the park visitor stamps that Americans collect when they visit parks in their national system as a rare souvenir of a visit to one of the least visited US national parks.

As our time was pressing, we decided to drive into the northern reaches of the park. We drove over Route No. 001 east to Aua, where we connected to northbound Route No. 006 and ascended once again into Tutuila's mountainous rainforest on a well-paved road. We had been told that there was a turn-off high in the mountains that gave a very picturesque view of Pola Island, which is one of the most magnificent natural features in American Samoa, so we made sure to pull over into the turn-off when we found it. It seems that everyone who visits Tutuila stops to take a photograph of Pola Island. Pola is a high cliff wedge island lying just off the north shore of Tutuila and it is a sanctuary for many species of oceanic birds that can nest on Pola in relative safety. At one time in the distant past young men on Tutuila scaled the cliffs of Pola to demonstrate their manhood and their courage as a rite of passage into manhood.

The often-photographed landmark of Pola Island

Pola Island is a favoured nesting place for oceanic birds

Here in the rainforest, I became aware of many birds chirping and singing, though all of them remained concealed from me in the dense vegetation. I did, however, discover two of the reptile species on Tutuila there at the National Park site, a gecko, and a small skink, both of which froze their motion when I first looked at them. Each of them scampered away when my gaze went elsewhere.

Eventually, as we drove on from the turn-off site, the road descended from the mountains and we found ourselves once again on the coast, now at the north side where we drove as far as the end of the road at the village of Vatia to obtain a closer look at Pola. At Vatia our attention was also caught by a large sign at the beach that warned us of a shark sighting and advised against bathing in the ocean. This surprised us as there are few historical reports of shark attacks in American Samoan waters and the sign did not look like it was a temporary sign. Rather, it looked like a semi-permanent installation. Could it be, we wondered, that the villagers did not want visitors, especially scantily-clad visitors, swimming in the local waters? If so, a shark warning sign should certainly suffice to keep any uninformed scantily-clad visitor out of the water!

Shark Warning at Vatia!

The Natural Landmarks

The US National Park Service has a program to identify significant natural landmarks in the United States and its outlying territories and seven such natural landmarks have been identified in American Samoa. Most of the Natural Landmarks of American Samoa are actually outside the boundaries of the National Park itself. First and foremost among the great natural landmarks on Tutuila Island are the two towering mountains that guard each side of Pago Pago Harbour, Rainmaker Mountain (Mount Pioa) the mountain that is largely responsible for the heavy annual rainfall received in the harbour, and Mount Matafao, the highest point on Tutuila. In the north, Vai'ava Strait, which includes the magnificent Pola Island is named Natural Landmark, and in the east, the entire island of Aunu'u is also named because of its relatively recent volcanic flows, and the effects of erosion. The final three landmarks are all in the west of Tutuila and consist of Cape Taputapu at the western extremity of the island, the Fogama'a Crater adjacent to the Fogama'a sector of the National Marine Sanctuary of American Samoa, and finally the Le'ala Shoreline at Leone, another example of basalt volcanic flows and erosion effects.

Vai'ava Strait, a Natural Landmark of American Samoa

Flora and Fauna of the Islands

As befits a country possessed of a natural rainforest and offshore coral reefs American Samoa has a great variety of species of animals and plants. The greatest diversity is to be found offshore, in the waters of the South Pacific, where upwards of 1000 different species of fish and other marine life may be found. Most impressive among the marine specimens are the Humpback Whales, which annually visit American Samoan waters in September and October. Pilot Whales, Dolphins, and Porpoises are also found in American Samoan waters, as is the occasional Sperm Whale. The impressive Coconut Crab, the world's largest marine arthropod is also found in American Samoa.

Onshore there are two species of flying foxes, the Samoan Flying Fox and the White Collared Flying Fox, which are the only native mammals in American Samoa. Reptiles are represented by the gecko and the skink, and on Ta'u Island, the Pacific Boa Constrictor, while two marine turtles, the Green Turtle, and rare Hawksbill Turtle, occasionally visit land in American Samoa. There is a rich variety of bird life with many oceanic birds nesting in the islands (Pola Island is a particular hotspot for marine bird life) and a careful observer at the appropriate time of year may see petrels, shearwaters, terns, boobies, curlews, and the frigate bird. There are also many native birds in the rainforest, including kingfishers, fruit doves, pigeons, honeyeaters, Samoan Starlings, and the Blue-Crowned Lorikeet. The Barn Owl is the only terrestrial bird of prey. The Manumea, or Tooth-Billed Pigeon was once found on Tutuila but it has now been extirpated.

In addition to the native species, there are several introduced and invasive species in American Samoa, such as the marine toad, the common rat, snails, ants, mosquitos, and feral pigs. One introduced animal that is present in large numbers is the dog, which probably came with the original settlers to the Samoan Archipelago two or three millennia ago. Dogs in American Samoa are known to be aggressive towards people that they are unfamiliar with. Although many dogs appear to be free-roaming a brochure from the Visitor's Bureau assures that many dogs do belong to residents. However, some dogs probably do not and others being free-ranging are perhaps a little more feral than the dogs one is generally accustomed to seeing in North America. Caution is therefore indicated whenever dogs are present, a message that was reinforced by the pamphlet I received from the Visitor's Bureau before we visited the islands. I was always careful to look to see if any dogs were about when exiting our vehicle in a more remote setting. Because dogs are more free-ranging on Tutuila it was also important to keep an eye out for them on the road, although dogs on Tutuila seem generally smart enough to keep out of harm's way while they are on the road. The low-speed limit in American Samoa also offers dogs on the road some protection from the danger of moving vehicles.

Chickens are also an introduced animal and we encountered some feral or semi-feral chickens while hiking but in comparison to Hawaii, and especially the Hawaiian Island of Kauai, there are far fewer wild chickens on Tutuila than on Hawaii's Garden Island.

The rainforests of Tutuila and the dense vegetation of Aunu'u contain a wide variety of native flora and some other popular tropical flowers have also been introduced into the environment. Flowering Ginger and Frangipani, or Plumeria, are often seen (the Frangipani is particularly seen in the hair of women as an accoutrement) and orchids also grow here. More than a thousand species of plants can be found in American Samoa.

Flowering Ginger

As we drove south through the Amalau Valley from Pola Island on Route No. 005, we kept a lookout for flying foxes as we had learned that the Samoan Flying Fox at least, is active during the day. Sure enough, Vi spied two of the bats winging over the valley although, as I was driving, they were a little too quick for me to see them. We came down out of the mountains and returned to Tafuna.

11

A Visit to Government House

During our visit to American Samoa, we were privileged to obtain a private visit to Government House, the seat of executive power in the country. Government House, also known as *Maugaoalii* in the Samoan language, is the official residence of the Governor and First Lady of American Samoa. The building is listed on the US National Register of Historic Places and is intimately connected to the history of the United States' involvement in the islands. Our visit to Government House was arranged through the efforts of Ms. Orepa Rosery Talo, the Executive Assistant to the First Lady of American Samoa, and with the kind permission of the First Lady herself, Her Excellency Ella Mauga, the wife of Governor His Excellency High Chief Lemanu Peleti Mauga.

Government House on Observatory Point in Utulei

Government House is a very prominent and historic building on the island. Perched atop Observatory Point in the Utulei village within the Greater Pago Pago urban area the structure has been the residence of the Governors of American Samoa since the early twentieth century. At first, after the United States asserted its sovereignty over Tutuila and Aunu'u in 1900, the Commandants of the US Naval Station Tutuila resided aboard the station ship assigned to the islands by the US Navy. Thus, the first Commandant, Commander Benjamin F. Tilley maintained his headquarters aboard his command vessel, the USS *Abarenda* although he also maintained a small office ashore. Civil government during this period was largely left in the hands of the *Matai*. In 1901, Tilley was succeeded as US Naval Commandant by Captain U. Segree who also stayed aboard the USS *Abarenda*, serving as its commanding officer as well as administering the islands as had Commander Tilley. In 1902, the US Naval Commandant at Tutuila was relieved of the duty of also commanding the station ship allowing the naval commandants to direct their energies exclusively to the affairs of the naval station and the governance of the islands. It was Segree who received orders from the navy to construct an official residence for the Governor of the islands. Although Segree himself was not officially appointed as Governor he began to be informally described as the Governor of the islands.

Segree instructed one of his junior officers, Ensign Bloch, to construct an official residence on Observatory Point, which is a high point above Pago Pago Harbour, a placement that would emphasize the status of the American governors to the Samoans. The location on Observatory Point also gave magnificent views of Pago Pago Harbour and the naval establishments on land, thus allowing the naval governors to watch over their military domain. Extensive site engineering was required before construction could actually begin on a structure however, as Bloch had to reduce the grade on Observatory Point from 25 metres to 20 metres to obtain the ground footprint size that he wanted for a large mansion.

The Navy hired two highly qualified carpenters from California to oversee the construction of the house and local labour was engaged to undertake the work. The building was designed by naval architects and constructed as a frame and weather-boarded two-story cross-shaped mansion with attic dormers, a corrugated metal roof, and extensive covered verandahs. The whole structure was secured on concrete piers fastened by metal rods to obtain stability in the event of cyclones. The architectural style chosen for Government House by its architects was that of a Tropical Victorian variation of the Greek Revival architectural style that was then popular in America. The Greek Revival style emphasized well-defined shapes, clean lines, and a lack of architectural ostentation. The Tropical Victorian variation incorporated sunshades, overhangs, and a two-story verandah that wrapped around most of the mansion. Natural shading is a feature of the Tropical Victorian style and, in 1914, the then Governor ordered a major landscaping project for all of Observatory Point. More than 1500 trees and plants were planted at Observatory Point, including mango, papaya, avocado, kapok, candlenut, coconut, breadfruit, and shade trees.

The mansion was pierced by many windows owing to the hot climate and, of course, there was no need for any cold-weather insulation or heating. The building has always been painted white, perhaps a subtle comparison to the executive mansion of the United States in Washington, which is also white. The size of the structure is approximately 38 metres by 23 metres for a total area of 966 square metres, or 10,400 square feet. Thus a truly massive home was built for the US Naval Governors and one that was probably intended to impress the Samoans with the might and power of the United States.

Government House

Over time changes were made to Government House and there were additions as well as enclosures of some portions of the extensive verandahs. Some outbuildings were also constructed such as a storage facility, a carport, and a ceremonial pavilion in a traditional Samoan design. A steep 146-metre paved driveway leads from Route No 001 up the hillside to the Government House grounds and a zigzagging staircase was built up the hillside from the highway to the lawn of Government House that once afforded pedestrian access from the coastal road. A formal white wooden fence surrounds the grounds and walkways have been built along the interior of the fence line.

Interior walkways have been constructed along the fence line

Our visit was planned for 9:00 A.M. on our last day in American Samoa. We left our hotel on that day somewhat earlier than we had usually gone out on other days but not early enough because I did not foresee that there would be traffic congestion on Tutuila in the mornings. I learned that despite being a paradise Tutuila has a morning traffic jam. I was concerned that we might be late for our tour but in the end, we made it with a few minutes to spare and I parked our truck in the parking lot at the Ocean Centre, as I had been warned that there was no public parking at Government House.

Earlier in our explorations of the island, we had noted the position of Government House high on its hilltop above the harbour and I had also spied the elaborate concrete staircase that went up the hillside. Thinking that the staircase would be a fairly easy way to reach Government House we went up the stairs only to find that a gate at the top was bolted shut and there was no access from the stairs. So back down we went and we then walked along the coastal road to the point where the Government House driveway meets Route No. 001. There we found a guardhouse and the guard came out to greet us. We were expected and that's when I found out that I could have parked our vehicle at the guardhouse since we were expected guests.

The guard radioed up the mansion to say that we were here and he offered to arrange for a car to take us up the hill. However, we decided that we would walk up the driveway to Government House rather than put anyone to the trouble of conveying us. The guard warned us however that we might encounter free-roaming dogs and to be aware of that. Thus warned, we went up the hillside without incident and we were greeted at the top by Ms. Talo and a fine-bearing older gentleman whom she simply introduced to us as "the Major," and who was the head of security for Government House. When introducing us she told us that the Major was soon to retire after serving in the local American Samoan police force for a total of 50 years. The Major and his aide also accompanied us on the tour.

After introductions were complete Ms. Talo gave us a brief tour of the grounds of Government House. Initially, she pointed to the small building further back from where we stood which she explained was a ceremonial structure that has often been used by the First Ladies of American Samoa to host ladies' events. We then walked around two sides of the imposing Government

House itself. As we did so, Ms. Talo pointed to the second story where a balustrade seemed to be rather incongruously erected against an exterior wall. However, Ms. Talo explained that what we were looking at was one of the original upper-story verandahs that had been subsequently enclosed without removing the original balustrade. I could well imagine what it had originally looked like and I envisaged a US Naval Governor in the early days of the colony looking out from that vantage point over the ships at anchor in the harbour.

The original second-story verandah has been enclosed leaving the original balustrade as an external feature

We had walked around the house to where a grass lawn stretched from the house to the gate where we had been stopped earlier when we had tried to enter the grounds through the staircase that reached up from the road below to the Government House grounds. Here, Ms. Talo pointed out the spectacular views of Pago Pago Harbour and Rainmaker Mountain. I imagined evenings from another age when naval governors in their starched white uniforms sat on the upper verandah overlooking the harbour sipping mint juleps while their chatelaines sat with them.

A verandah where naval governors once sat with their chatelaines

Rainmaker Mountain from the Governor's garden

After our brief tour of the grounds, we entered the mansion into the formal sitting room, which Ms. Talo told us was not a part of the original building but was a subsequent addition. Large windows along the wall bathed the room in light and the room was comfortably appointed, accented by a tiled floor and some elaborate woodwork that showcased the local carving expertise available on Tutuila. Nearby photographs showed us what this room originally looked like. In the days of the naval governors and afterward, this large room was used to display artifacts from the culture of American Samoa. However, a Governor in the early seventies, John Morse Haydon, established a museum in honour of his wife, Jean P. Haydon, and the artifacts that were housed at Government House were transferred to the new museum as the basis for its collection of Samoan culture. Afterwards, this room became the formal sitting room at Government House.

The formal sitting room at Government House

The sitting room as it looked in the days of the naval governors

Next, we visited the combined library and study of the Governor. The library was lined with bookshelves filled with US law books, a legacy of a former governor who had been a lawyer in private life. There were also traditional artifacts from Samoan culture, including some reproduced weapons from the days of clan warfare on the islands. Ms. Talo explained that in earlier times various chiefs and high chiefs would strive through warfare to secure the position of king in the islands, and thus inter-island and inter-village conflict was a constant. Such conflicts ended when the Samoan Archipelago was partitioned by Germany and the United States.

Modern replicas of traditional Samoan arms

We also viewed several examples of American football memorabilia, as the current Governor is a football fan. Centred in the room was the Governor's desk and behind the Governor's desk was a leather-bound chair. Flanking the Governor's desk were the flags of the United States and American Samoa. Opposite the Governor's desk and chair was a shelf or table upon which there were a monitor and webcams. Ms. Talo explained that when necessary the Governor would make televised addresses to the people of American Samoa from this room.

The Governor's Study at Government House

A traditional war club

In the hallway outside of the library, we examined some historical photographs of Government House, including a photograph of the original architectural plans by the US Navy, and another early photo showing a landslide below Government House before the slope of Observatory Point was protected by stabilization measures as part of the 1914 landscaping project. Another historical photograph showed a former First Lady holding tea in the separate traditional pavilion outside next to the mansion.

A fourth historical photograph showed the former Goat Island in Pago Pago Harbour and the causeway that once linked Goat Island to Tutuila. The photograph of Goat Island prompted Ms. Talo to relate to us the important story of how the Spanish Influenza was prevented from gaining a foothold in the American Samoan islands in 1918. Goat Island, lying in Pago Pago harbour, was established as a quarantine site early in the American administration of the islands and was used on a few occasions for that purpose before World War One. Late in World War One an influenza pandemic known to history as the Spanish Influenza emerged and raced around the world spreading high mortality wherever it reached. On Tutuila, the American naval Governor, Commander John Poyer, learned of the pandemic from wireless transmissions and, acting on his own authority, he took extreme measures to protect the islands of American Samoa from the pandemic. Passengers and crew on incoming ships were quarantined, many of them on Goat Island, to prevent the introduction of the Spanish Influenza into the country. The *Matais* were persuaded to patrol their areas of the coastline to prevent any landings from the indigenous residents of neighbouring German Samoa, which was then under New Zealand occupation and administration. In Samoa, the disease was allowed to be introduced and to spread widely, as a result of the negligence of the New Zealand occupation authorities. Because of Governor Poyer's initiative, no residents of American Samoa were infected with the influenza and the country became one of the very few places in the world that were spared the depredations of the outbreak. In contrast, occupied German Samoa suffered a 20% mortality rate, permanently staining the reputation of its New Zealand occupiers. In American Samoa, a local school was subsequently named after Governor Poyer, in recognition of his efforts to prevent the advance of the disease into American Samoa. As for Goat Island, it was later the site of a club for naval officers but afterwards the causeway was expanded with fill and the island became a peninsula.

Goat Island in former days

Moving along on our tour we entered the main reception foyer where an elegant staircase led up to the private apartments of the Governor's family. In the foyer, we admired some of the photographs and artifacts on display. There was a large carved wooden slit drum near the staircase. At first, I was not sure what it was but Ms. Talo explained that the slit drum was a traditional device that took the place of a bell and was used for several purposes including school assembly and marking the beginning and end of *Sa*, the period of vespers mandated each day in some of the villages on the islands. In addition to war clubs, there were two different types of fish traps on display, a hand-woven funnel trap called an *enu*, which is still used in the Manu'a Islands, and another cylindrical fish trap. Such traps allow fish to enter but not to leave. Another object that attracted my attention was a large carved wooden paddle mounted on the wall and I learned that it was a gift to American Samoa from the people of the Cook Islands that lie to the east of American Samoa in the South Pacific. As for the walls themselves, I remarked to our hostess that I had seen the same Dutch Lap style of construction when we briefly visited the High Court of Justice and she remarked that the style of construction represented the preferred naval style in the early twentieth century period.

A slit drum was used to mark the beginning and end of Sa

A carved wooden panel was a gift from the Cook Islands

The cylindrical fish trap

The last room on our tour of the public rooms at Government House was the state dining room. The formal dining room can seat twenty-four guests at table and its walls also displayed some of the traditional Samoan weaponry we had seen elsewhere in the mansion. This room would have been the centre of American naval diplomacy in the South Pacific during the years in which the US Navy ruled the islands. The first official state dinner at Government House occurred in April 1904, when Governor Underwood entertained Dr. Wilhelm Solf, the Governor of German Samoa. Over the years other colonial governors, especially the governors of the neighbouring German colony would have been entertained here, and later, during the inter-war years, there were visits by prominent Americans, and by foreign military officers and distinguished statesmen. Among those known to have been entertained here by the US naval governors were the Governors-General of New Zealand, Australian Premiers, US Congressmen, and US Navy Admirals.

The State Dining Room at Government House

In the modern era, following the initiation of self-government in 1978, and especially following the inauguration of the first elected indigenous Governor, state dinners and other formal entertainments at Government House now reflect the requisites of the local government, and the sentiments of the indigenous population.

Detail from Government House correspondence, circa 1950

We expressed our thanks and appreciation to our hosts for a very informative tour of this historic mansion, and we left to prepare for our departure from the islands later that day.

12

The Islands We Missed -- The Outer Islands

Our trip to American Samoa was a short one and disappointingly we were not able to visit all of the islands of American Samoa. The mountainous Manu'a Islands of Ta'u, Ofu, and Olosega lie about 100 kilometres to the east of Tutuila and Aunu'u Islands and their remoteness means that they are even more laid back and quiet than the main island of Tutuila. Much of those islands, especially Ta'u, have been leased to the National Park Service and form part of the National Park of American Samoa. These islands are sparsely inhabited and even more socially conservative than Tutuila or Aunu'u Islands.

Ta'u Island, the largest of the group, is famous among Polynesians as the heart of Polynesia. According to legend, it was the Polynesian god Tagaloa who looked down from the heavens and commanded the creation of Ta'u and the other Manu'a Islands. In the West, Ta'u is remembered as the site of the groundbreaking early twentieth-century anthropological work by famed American anthropologist Margaret Mead, who published her most famous book, *Coming of Age in Samoa*, in 1925. Finally, Ta'u is also notable because it is the habitat of the only resident terrestrial snake in American Samoa, the relatively harmless Pacific Boa Constrictor.

Ofu Island is famous for its long white sand beach. The unspoiled beach on Ofu Island has often been hailed as one of the most beautiful beaches in the Pacific Ocean, if not in the entire world. The beach and a portion of the offshore area are now protected as part of the National Park of American Samoa.

Ofu Beach

Picturesque Maga Point on Olosega is known for its spectacular views of the ocean and of neighbouring Ta'u Island. Since the 1930's an air service has linked the Manu'a Islands with Tutuila and flights to both Ta'u and Ofu are available from Tutuila, while it is possible to hire a boat to travel between Ta'u and Olosega.

A local stamp marking the 1931 start of airmail to the Manu'a Islands

American Samoa also includes two small atolls, Rose Atoll and Swains Island. Rose Atoll is uninhabited and is one of the smallest atolls in the world but it is very important from a natural perspective. Rose is an important atoll for nesting birds and most of the oceanic bird species native to American Samoa nest on Rose Atoll. Sea turtles, including the rare Hawksbill Turtle, also come to Rose Atoll to lay their eggs. Consequently, Rose Atoll was declared to be a US National Wildlife Reserve in the twentieth century. In 2009, the atoll and its surrounding waters were also included in the National Marine Monument of American Samoa and the upshot of all of those protective measures is that tourism is prohibited on Rose Atoll. Permission must be obtained to visit the atoll, and permission may be only granted to scientists who are conducting scientific research involving Rose Atoll.

Swains Island is also unique but mostly for historical reasons. The atoll was purchased by a member of an American family, the Jennings, in the nineteenth century from a British sea captain who evidently had, or thought he had, some colour of right to assert title to the atoll. Thereafter, the Jennings family ruled the island as a kind of private fiefdom. Eventually, the United States annexed the island in 1925 (with the agreement of the Jennings family) and the US left the Jennings family in charge of it, although the atoll was made part of the US Territory of America Samoa. At the time there was, and had been for a long period, a coconut plantation on the atoll. The Copra plantation on Swains Island mostly used imported labour from what was then called the Union Islands but which are now called the Tokelau Islands, the island group that lies north of American Samoa. A labour dispute in the early 1950s led the Governor of American Samoa to establish a local government on Swains Island and to provide for the representation of Swains Islanders in the American Samoan Fono.

In recent years economic conditions have led to the closure of the copra plantation on the atoll and most of the inhabitants, many of them contract workers, have left the island. The 2020 US census listed no permanent inhabitants on the island. However, Swains Island continues to be owned by the Jennings family and it is the Jennings family that represents the interests of the island in the American Samoan Fono. It is very difficult to arrange to visit this atoll but apparently, it is possible to do so with the permission of the Jennings family.

Swains Island was the subject of a marine documentary by Jean-Michel Cousteau, the son of the famous French oceanographer, Jacques Cousteau, who extolled its marine uniqueness.

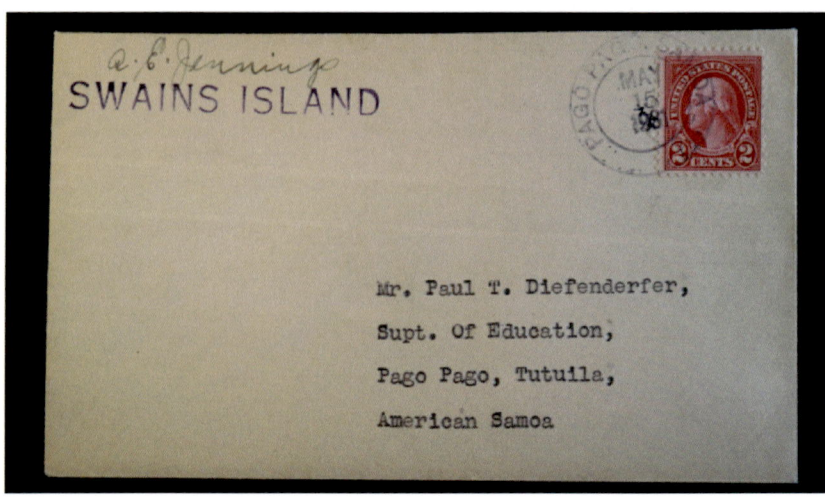

A rare example from postal history: a letter from Swains Island circa 1931

13

Departing American Samoa

Our departure from American Samoa was largely uneventful. We checked in with Hawaiian Airlines for our trip back to Hawaii and sat in the open-air *fale* waiting area until the Immigration Office opened, and we could obtain our exit visas. Once that was done we were able to pass through security and enter the air-conditioned departure lounge to await the arrival of the aeroplane from Hawaii.

The only misadventure we encountered concerned Vi's determination to take with her to Hawaii a green papaya that she had obtained on Tutuila. I warned her that Hawaii and American Samoa were separate customs jurisdictions and that the customs authorities in Honolulu would doubtless relieve her of her papaya but she thought otherwise since the American flag flew over both islands. Alas for her I was right, and upon our arrival the US customs declared her papaya to be contraband and seized it, dashing my wife's hopes for a nice homemade papaya salad on the island of Kauai!

The Present and Future of American Samoa

American Samoa currently enjoys a privileged position in the South Pacific. It is part of, and yet not part of, the United States of America. It is both American and it is also its own country. It enjoys a democratic form of government that is based on an American model but which also differs from the American model in particular aspects. For American Samoans to have survived a long period under American military and civilian rule and to have ultimately emerged into a state of indigenous self-government has been a fortunate circumstance. It was a result that escaped the Hawaiians, the only other Polynesian people to fall under the sway of the United States. Locals in American Samoa with whom we discussed the comparison between American Samoa and Hawaii told us that while the Polynesian culture had remained strong in American Samoa "in Hawaii they keep trying to hold on to the culture but it still keeps fading away."

But American Samoans have had an advantage that Hawaiians never had and that is the neighbouring presence of independent Samoa, which shares the same language and the same culture as American Samoa, and which can replenish American Samoa both culturally and demographically. While some traditional skills may have diminished in American Samoa, Samoan cultural knowledge and traditional skills remain in neighbouring Samoa, and the people of American Samoa can rely upon their neighbour as a sort of cultural repository. Immigration from Samoa into

American Samoa has also helped to replenish the population where demographic declines might otherwise have denuded the islands of their population, since many who have been born in the territory have exercised their rights as American Nationals to relocate to the United States, generally in search of better economic outcomes.

Officials I met assured me during our visit that there was no desire among the population of American Samoa to seek independence from the United States. In fact, the major secular holiday in American Samoa is Flag Day, April 17th, which is the anniversary of the day the American flag was first raised on Tutuila. On that day the American Samoan people display their loyalty to the United States in speeches and special flag-raising ceremonies. For the present, at least, the political *status quo* seems to be favoured by the people of American Samoa.

The existence of American sovereignty over the islands forestalls any external threats to American Samoa, and American Samoa's position in the southeastern quadrant of the Pacific Ocean places it among friendly pro-western neighbours. To the west is Samoa with which American Samoa shares both a language and a culture. To the north and south are the New Zealand dependencies of the Tokelau Islands and Niue, respectively. To the east are the Cook Islands, which is an associated state of New Zealand, and further east is French Polynesia, an overseas country of France, and then, farthest east are the Pitcairn Islands, a British colony.

The status of American Samoans as American Nationals, rather than US citizens, reflects the island's history as an unorganised and unincorporated possession of the United States but it has also served to protect the unique culture and political institutions of this small country. The US Congress did not impose a US Organic Act on American Samoa leaving open an avenue for the American Samoans to design public institutions for the territorial government that were compatible with *Fa'a Samoa*, including the ability to preserve the communal landholding structure that was essential to maintaining indigenous control of the lands on the islands. Whether further integration with the United States would lead to a loss of the political structures built around the *Matai* and a loss of the communal landholding system, are open questions. Some legal scholars, in particular, have pointed to the nobility clause of the US Constitution as a barrier to the continuation of the hold of the *Matai* on particular American Samoan political institutions should integration proceed.

In recent years there have been rumblings of discontent in some quarters about the continuing status of an American National for those who are born in the islands. Officials with whom I spoke about this issue recognise that a driver for this issue is the special bond that many American Samoans feel towards the US military. It is a fact that a higher proportion of the American Samoan population serves in the American military than the populations of other US territories or US states. We were told that both the current Governor and the First Lady were US military veterans, as are many American Samoans in the islands. Strong encouragement is given to American Samoan youth to consider careers in the US military. Around the time of our visit, I noted that an American Samoan woman who was serving in the US forces, and who had obtained the senior enlisted rank of Command Master Chief Petty Officer in the US Navy, was scheduled to make several public engagements, including speaking at schools. Although there is a pathway for American Samoans who join the US forces to obtain American citizenship some of those who serve and place themselves in potential jeopardy have wondered why they do not automatically enjoy American citizenship.

Additionally, those American Samoans who have permanently, or perhaps semi-permanently, moved to the US mainland are also among those who have called for the conversion of their status from American Nationals to American Citizens, so that they might vote in US elections on the American mainland, and enjoy the other benefits of US citizenship.

In this century two cases have been lodged in US federal courts that sought declarations that all people born in the territory of American Samoa were entitled to a birthright US citizenship; *Tuaua v. United States*, and *Fitisemanu v. United States*. Both cases were dismissed at the federal appellate court level, and the Supreme Court of the United States denied appeal applications in both instances. Perhaps wisely, the Supreme Court recognized that any change in the status of American Samoans was essentially a political question that was best left to the American Samoan *Fono*, the American Samoan executive, and the US Congress to resolve.

American Samoa controls its own borders and does not currently face any external challenges. Although the decision of neighbouring Western Samoa to formally change its name from Western Samoa to The Independent State of Samoa in 1997, was briefly protested by American Samoa because it was thought that it might diminish American Samoa's identity the original name of Western Samoa was anomalous because no entity was called Eastern Samoa. In any event, the name change rationalised Samoa's official name with the name under which it had joined the United Nations in the mid-Seventies, and it was not viewed in Washington as a potential territorial claim by Samoa over American Samoa.

There was a brief contretemps in 2006-07 involving Swains Island and the Tokelau Islands, a dependency of New Zealand. In 1981, the United States and New Zealand (with the support of the then-political leadership of the Tokelau Islands) entered into a treaty the terms of which required the United States to surrender all of its claims to the Tokelau Islands in return for New Zealand surrendering any sovereignty claim to Swains Island (which is geographically part of the Tokelau Islands group). Subsequent public sentiment in the Tokelau Islands became unreconciled to the perceived loss of Swains Island. When, in the course of the political evolution of the Tokelau Islands a new flag for the dependency was proposed, the flag that was chosen showed Swains Island as part of the Tokelau Islands. That action was perceived as a potential sovereignty claim and action was taken to require revision to the flag to ensure that it could not be seen to be a sovereignty claim in violation of the 1981 treaty. Nevertheless, this issue, while now dormant, could erupt again into a transnational issue in the future if either Tokelau or American Samoa were to become independent states.

A larger external issue currently facing many Pacific island countries is the international competition between the United States and the rising power of China in the Pacific Ocean. The United States has large strategic interests in the Pacific Ocean and it has been the naval master of the Pacific since the defeat of Japan in 1945. However, the rise of China in the post-Mao-Tse-Tung era compelled the United States to adjust to the growing military might of China in the western Pacific. The most important strategic interests of the United States in the Western Pacific involve the protection of Japan, Korea, and the Philippines, as well as American support for democratic Taiwan, and the free passage of ships through the South China Sea. US naval and military strategy in the Pacific has been centred on anchoring its defences around three distant island chains to prevent China from encroaching into the sphere of American hegemony in the Pacific. Under the island chain defence theory, America must maintain control over all three island chains to contain China in the Pacific Ocean.

The first island chain running from north to south consists of Japan, Taiwan, the Philippines and Borneo, the latter an island divided between Malaysia, Brunei, and Indonesia. The second island chain begins in the north with Japan's Bonin and Volcano Islands and extends south through the US territories of the Commonwealth of the Northern Mariana Islands, and Guam, proceeds through the western Caroline Islands of the independent Federated States of Micronesia, then the independent Palau Islands, and reaches south to its terminus on the island of New Guinea, an island divided between Indonesia and Papua New Guinea. The third island chain running north to south consists of the American-owned Aleutian Islands of Alaska, the Hawaiian Islands, American Samoa, and then onwards to independent Fiji and New Zealand. As can be seen, American Samoa continues to provide a strategic resource to the US military as part of the third island chain, although American Samoa remains far from the current main area of contention in the western Pacific.

The crux of the challenge for the United States is that China has built the world's largest blue-water fleet and all of it is stationed in East Asia, while the US Navy is scattered worldwide with global responsibilities. That allows China to achieve naval dominance in the western Pacific. The predicament facing the US Navy is similar to that faced by Great Britain before World War One when Imperial Germany built a large fleet that it based in the North Sea while Britain's Royal Navy maintained ships across its vast empire to keep international sea lanes open. Added to the conundrum facing the US Navy are the new aircraft carriers China is building and deploying, with three expected to be operational by the mid-2020s that will give Chinese naval power an extended reach in the Pacific Ocean.

But perhaps the largest external challenge faced by American Samoa is one that equally affects all island countries in particular, and that is climate change. The threat posed to island communities and cultures by a warming planet is a very real one. The melting of the polar ice caps and the resulting increase in sea levels could swamp some small island countries outright. Although most of American Samoa is mountainous, and therefore impervious to swamping, most of its people live along coastal plains and some part of the population might be forced to relocate away from rising seas.

As for the true future of American Samoa, only time will tell, of course, but one can only hope that these beautiful islands with their friendly people will continue to enjoy the best of both the Western and Oceanic worlds.

www.ingramcontent.com/pod-product-compliance
Lightning Source LLC
Chambersburg PA
CBRC091722070526
44585CB00007B/145